Restoring Junk

Written and illustrated by
SUZANNE BEEDELL
MOLLIE

With the editorial assistance of
BARBARA HARGREAVES

Foreword by
JOHN BEDFORD

DAVID McKAY COMPANY, INC.
NEW YORK

First Published in 1970
First American Edition in 1971
Manufactured in Great Britain

CONTENTS

FOREWORD

Anyone who has spent much time looking in junk shops will know that sooner or later a particular decision will have to be made. Is one to insist on buying only the perfect piece, the flawless jewel, which has come down to our time unscathed by time—that enemy of both man and his handiwork? Or is one to be content with something less than perfection, that which is flawed—though not irreparably?

If you take the first course and happen to have a taste for the best in furniture, pictures, pottery, glass, silver, or whatever, you will nowadays need a very long purse indeed. The fine things of the seventeenth and eighteenth centuries have soared in price to levels which would not have been thought possible even only five years ago. In the meantime collectors have turned their attention to the once despised nineteenth century; and Victoriana is now as eagerly accepted for sale by great auctioneers like Sotheby's and Christie's as anything of earlier date.

Personally I have never felt especially impressed by 'condition' for its own sake. If a piece is what the trade calls 'right'—that is to say genuine of its own kind, if whatever imperfections it may have do not seriously detract from enjoyment of it, I do not see why it should not take its place in a collection. After all, for a piece of china or furniture to have survived for two hundred, a hundred, or even fifty years without acquiring some sort of blemish, or show some signs of age, is a quite remarkable thing: it has certainly not happened to me. One suspects too, that those who seek perfection of this kind may be interested not so much in the appreciation of a particular *objet d'art*, as in appreciation of their investment—and I have always thought that there were many pitfalls in that kind of collecting.

A few years ago there came up for sale a famous collection of teapots, representative of the finest work of all the famous English factories. The reverend gentleman who put it together, however, could not possibly have afforded to do so had he not been content to accept the odd chip, crack or restored part. But these imperfections in no way spoilt the beauty and interest of the collection, which, though unique of its kind, had much instructive value for the general collector.

For me, therefore, if a piece has been skilfully and sympathetically repaired, with awareness of period and of the peculiar *nuances* of the original work, there would always be a place for it on my shelves or walls. And if you tell me that a repair or a repainting can be detected by ultra-violet radiation, I reply that one does not normally look at works of art through apparatus of that kind.

Before they buy, however, I think that collectors should inform themselves as to what can or cannot be done with anything which has been damaged or broken. Some things are really beyond all hope: they could never be restored in such a way as to give one the same kind of æsthetic appeal as the original, and the place for it—if there *is* a place for it—may well be in a museum. But there are many things which can be rescued, and ought to be before they deteriorate any further.

This, I think, is the value of a book like this. In showing how repairs can be done it tells one what repairs *can* be done, whether we do them ourselves with loving care or whether we leave them to the expert. There are not so many fine works of art about that we can afford to let them disappear without an effort of some sort.

John Bedford

INTRODUCTION

What is junk? Something which its last owner discarded as worthless? Any old piece of furniture, china, metalwork, any old picture, print or scrap which has no intrinsic value? These definitions have no meaning today when the trade in 'junk' has reached international proportions and when some of the prices paid for hideous bits of bric-a-brac put them far beyond the reach of most amateur collectors. Once, a poke around a second-hand shop produced all kinds of unusual and interesting things for shillings and even for pennies. Pounds didn't enter into it. Once you could go to auction sales and come away with car loads of discarded 'rubbish' which no one else at the sale wanted and for which the dealers, least of all the dealers, never bothered to bid.

Not any more. At every sale, in every junk shop, there lurks the man or woman with that indefinable look, that odd searching expression which proclaims that he or she is 'in the trade' and will buy all kinds of unlikely things just to turn them into other unlikely things or to restore them and sell them as totally genuine survivals from the past, and as always, when the dealers get interested the amateurs have to get up *very* early in the morning!

The reasons why we have come to value these things are strange, but fairly simple. As we invent new designs for furniture, pots and pans, clothes etc. and enjoy new styles and fashions, yesterday's style and the day before yesterday's become hideous to us. How ugly now seems the clothes and furniture, the carpets and curtains, the chairs and the pictures of the thirties. And how ugly, in the thirties, seemed the things we designed in the twenties. Yet now, in the sixties, the things of the twenties become attractive again, some of them, and the Victorian excesses which we hated in the thirties, positively delight us now. Why does this happen? Is it because our modern designs get more and more simple and functional, with fewer curves and fussy bits, more and more straight lines and flat surfaces, more and more synthetic finishes, and less and less craftsmanship or hand work of any kind is done. The horrors of photographic wood veneers, which only need a wipe with a damp cloth, the plastic 'working' surfaces which every knife marks, are preferred to beautiful natural veneers which need a bit of polishing to keep them beautiful, and to scrubbed wood which needs a bit of elbow grease to keep it clean. So I believe some of us are coming to value the things which man has made with his hands out of natural materials as an antidote to our machine-turned, moulded, plastic world. And I don't believe that the plastic rubbish of today will ever become the treasured junk of tomorrow or the day after tomorrow. We have gone right over the top, and many people are determined to salve what is left of the artifacts of our grandfathers. The very ugliness of some of the things has the appeal of individuality at the least. It may be claimed that a lot of Victorian and Edwardian and even Georgian junk was mass produced in the sense that numbers of copies of the same objects were made, and that any casting or turning or moulding techniques that were available were fully used. Nevertheless the materials themselves ensured that hand finishing was almost always necessary, and the machines were worked by men and not by other machines. Designs were made by the minds of men and not by computers.

Ingenious people go to great lengths to make modern objects out of old junk, sometimes by taking things back to an even more original condition than they ever were before, when they were first made. I'm thinking of the vogue for stripping down wooden objects and oiling or waxing so that the grain alone decorates them; objects that were always stained or painted when they were first produced. It is only quite recently that we have realised that natural pine wood can be just as beautiful as natural walnut, or oak or mahogany. Our immediate forefathers thought that pine in its natural state was very ugly and only fit to be covered up. Anyone who had ever visited an alpine country knew differently, but nevertheless we remained very traditional. Taking the subject a stage further, there was a time when natural oak furniture was looked upon as being purely rural and only used by the yokels in the kitchen, and nothing could be elegant but inlaid mahogany or veneer or ormolu. All kinds of objects get turned into lamps nowadays, and old picture frames make fine mirrors and trays. Pianos turn into cocktail cabinets—there is a use for everything and anything. Is this because the hand craftsmanship, or even the time, that it takes to make these things cannot be found these days except at great expense? Labour was cheap when the junk was being made, and now we are taking advantage, years after the makers are dead and gone, of their sweated labour, their underpaid craftsmanship, which are just not available any more.

Lastly, as I discovered when I became involved in the art of restoring old cottages for modern living, you and I, amateurs in the sense that our jobs probably have nothing whatsoever to do with restoring things, get a great kick, an artistic satisfaction, out of mending something that seemed broken beyond repair, out of recreating something useful or decorative or interesting from something old, ugly and dull. The artist, the creator in all of us, can thus find expression even when we lack original talent. It may be in something as elemental as getting a good polish on a piece of filthy old brass.

Most of us are magpies at heart, and the collecting instinct which stimulates toddlers to collect little piles of stones, shells and sticks and string, the child to collect stamps or dolls and the teenager to collect gramophone records, stimulates the adult to collect whatever he or she can afford and finds pleasing. I know a man whose large Edwardian house (and he needs one) is full of musical boxes, everything from tiny little singing birds to huge great mahogany things which come to complicated life and give out fantastic sounds in response to the necessary stimuli. Another man will collect powder flasks, buttons or little boxes, or flatirons, or porcelain. Most collectors begin by acquiring a piece of junk almost accidentally, perhaps by inheritance, or bought in with an odd lot, or just because it caught the eye, and that is the nucleus of a collection.

People can be divided into two groups; those who will take everything to the 'expert' to be restored or cleaned, and those who will go to great lengths to do the work themselves. I think that the true junk collector comes into the second category. The greater part of the fun for him is in the restoring—in being able to say, modestly: 'yes, I mended that chair—it had three broken legs and six coats of paint, but the waxed natural wood does look rather nice, doesn't it?'

There are limitations, of course, on what can be done; limitations imposed by the necessity for expensive tools or materials, or processes which need equipment not usually found in even a well-equipped workshop (electro-plating tanks for instance). The one limitation that never seems to apply is that of knowledge, either of techniques or of materials.

Here another distinction has to be made. Properly speaking, restoration implies the recreating of an object so that it is exactly as it was when it was made. In the wider sense great arguments go on between the people and societies interested in the preservation of ancient things, and those who wish to restore them for actual use. To the purist, for instance, it is wrong when restoring a cottage to make structural alterations which are necessary to make it habitable in modern terms. To the purist it is wrong to restore an old piece of furniture by altering its original purpose, terrible to cut a whatnot in half and make two tables from it, even though it was useless as a whatnot. If a thing has intrinsic beauty then surely it is wrong to alter it out of recognition. There is a safeguard here in the sense that if you pay a lot of money for an antique you are unlikely to chop it about. On the other hand you might undervalue some inherited piece and destroy it by altering it.

How far is one justified in building up missing pieces of objects with modern epoxy resins instead of restoring the missing part as nearly as possible with its original material? Museums do it all the time and are prepared to rebuild and remake shamelessly with modern materials to restore objects, although they make no secret of this. It is of course impossible to lay down rules for these things. In any case the antique and junk trades are so full of fakes, composite objects, and reproductions with never any guarantee of authenticity, that it doesn't matter a great deal, I suppose, how authentic your restoration work on junk is. The only thing that matters, it seems to me, is that the reproduction or reconstruction or restoration produces something which as nearly resembles the original as one's capacities and the materials available allow. Never try to pass off any kind of restoration as original.

While in this book I have tried to include as many hints and ideas as possible, I have shied away from 'tricks of the trade'. There are too many tricksters about already.

Of course, with many perishable objects such as prints, preservation and protection against the ravages of the future is as important as restoration, and there seems to me to be no harm in using the most modern methods and materials available.

One or two general points must be made. First, that there s no substitute, really, for elbow grease, and this is in many cases the restorer's most useful material, substance or technique! It may be easy to slosh acids and solvents around, but the damage they do may well outweigh the time they save. Second, many chemicals used are poisonous or corrosive, and the greatest care must be taken when using them to wear protective clothing, gloves etc. Such materials should be confined to the workshop and never used in the kitchen. All bottles and jars must be carefully labelled, and poisons should be kept under lock and key. A fire extinguisher must be part of every workshop's equipment and a bucket of sand for extra fire protection isn't out of place. Plenty of fresh water should be available, and a sink is almost essential. Electrical equipment must be used properly and wall plugs etc. should be professionally installed and maintained. Never use electric tools with two-pin plugs. Use three-pin plugs which include an earth. Never unplug electrical equipment without first switching off the main. Never use electrical equipment with wet or even damp hands.

Lastly, I must point out that although all the recipes and suggestions in this book are tried and tested, the success of each and every one depends to some extent upon the user. It is like cooking. Give two people the same recipe book and materials and ask them to cook the same dish and the results will invariably differ.

Because of the enormous variety of materials involved, and because it is not possible for the writer to know exactly what it is that the reader is intending to treat, there can be no absolute certainty that methods and treatments will work exactly as planned. The contents of this book are meant as a guide, to be intelligently used. I have left out some techniques that call for the use of highly toxic chemicals (with the exception of the bleaching box), and I have left out or only briefly described techniques which do require practical instruction, although the borderline between skills which can be self-taught and developed by practice and those which have to be imparted on the spot by an expert, is impossible to define. It depends so much on the capacity and talent of the individual.

But it is junk you will be handling; it won't be world-shattering if you do make mistakes. There is so much pleasure in doing a good job that it is always worth a try. If you fail, well, that is too bad. If you succeed, that is wonderful, and oh, so satisfying.

Thanks. To write a book of this kind without picking other people's brains is impossible, for one cannot be an expert on everything; in fact the junk restorer must be a jack of all trades. Thanks are due, therefore, to all those who let me ask them questions about their working methods, and who gave me so much useful information. Thanks also to Ginette Leach whose help with the making and checking of the book was invaluable.

Using the book. The text is not divided into chapters, but set out with subjects in alphabetical order. I suggest that you look first in the indices for references to any specific subject, or material. There are two indices: the first refers specifically to materials and tools, and includes page references and names of suppliers and sources of the materials, so that in effect it replaces appendices; the second refers to the subject headings and methods, and is intended to lead you directly to the subject itself where you can find full details on cleaning and restoration.

Where various things come into the same general category they have been grouped together in that category rather than scattered through the book in alphabetical order. For instance the section headed Stone includes sub-sections of various kinds of stone. The sections on China, Furniture, and Metal are also comprehensive. This seems to me to be a more convenient way of arranging things than exact alphabetical order would have been.

The Art of Restoring

ABRASIVES

In order to remove rust, tarnish or corrosion from metal of all kinds, when soap and water, oil and paraffin mixture, rust removers, metal polishes, etc. have failed or are unsuitable, abrasives are used. In order to get a mirror finish on metal the correct use of the right abrasive is essential. To all intents and purposes, as they get finer, abrasives become polishes. Damaged woodwork can be cleaned and tidied with abrasives, stains and blooms on varnish can be removed; and used in conjunction with paints and varnishes, abrasives help to get deep glossy finishes.

As a general rule, work is started with coarse abrasives and finished with fine abrasives.

There are many different kinds of abrasives, and each user tends to prefer certain ones; it is not necessary to have all of them in your workshop. Abrasives can be bought in loose powder form, as cloth or paper, or in bar compositions for use with buffing tools.

For the purposes of this book it should be useful to describe briefly some of the abrasives and abrasive polishes available. In the various sections, abrasives are mentioned constantly in respect of specific uses. When working with them, trial and error is the best guide, provided that trials are not carried out on such a big scale that the error becomes irrevocable. After a while an invaluable experience of abrasives and their uses will be built up.

Abrasives such as sand and glasspaper, either in sheets or discs for power tools, are used for stripping down and smoothing wooden surfaces, and in conjunction with paint removers or by themselves, to remove stubborn old paint and varnish. When using sheet sandpaper, glasspaper or emery paper, it can be folded round blocks of wood, or made into sticks by wrapping round pieces of dowelling etc. Discs for sanders on power tools are made in a multitude of grades and qualities, some very rough indeed. Spaced grit carbide discs are excellent for tough work, where scoring of underlying wood can be removed at a later date. Metal discs with tungsten spaced grit over them are almost indestructible and will remove practically anything, but are liable to do damage as well, and should be used with great care.

Sheets of sand or glasspaper are used on finishing power sanders which do not revolve, but work with a fast backwards and forwards action.

Wet and dry emery paper in various grades, so called because it can be used dry or soaked in water as a lubricant without dissolving into pulp, will help to impart a mirror finish to any object which is being painted or varnished. The object is rubbed down with wet and dry between coats until the surface feels perfectly smooth to the fingertips. The emery is used very wet and the lubricating effect of the water helps the emery to cut smoothly without scratching.

Steel wool in various grades is a very versatile material. In rough grades, in conjunction with strippers, it will help to shift paint and varnish. Used with metal polishes it will remove stubborn stains on metals, and will help chemical rust removers to shift rust. Steel wool pads impregnated with soap are excellent for cleaning greasy metal or wood surfaces. Mirror finishes on wood can be rubbed down with fine steel wool, before waxing to achieve smooth shining but not over glossy finishes. The uses of steel wool in conjunction with wood finishing materials are many, and experience is invaluable. Grade 00 or 000 is used for fine work.

If you have a polishing lathe with interchangeable mops and brushes, or even if you set up a power drill to take small mops and bobs, you may wish to try liquid polishing compositions. These are equivalent to the bar compositions mentioned below and are intended to be sprayed on to the work as polishing is taking place. This requires special spray equipment so this method is usually only used commercially.

Emery powder, tripoli powder, rottenstone (a mineral found in Derbyshire and mixed with oil), jeweller's rouge (powdered iron oxide), pumice powder (powdered volcanic lava), crocus powder, carborundum, and whiting are all abrasives commonly used in metal finishing, and can be bought in composition bars, either greasy or non greasy, for use with polishing mops and brushes. They are used moistened on soft rags, or on swabs made up on sticks, or on small brushes (old toothbrushes come in handy here).

Obviously care must be taken not to use too strong an abrasive for your particular job. Do not risk making deep scratches which will need even deeper abrasion to be removed, and as polishing proceeds, use finer and finer abrasives until a deep glowing finish is achieved.

ACIDS

Some acids make effective cleaners. They should always be handled with care; rubber gloves must be worn, and the bottles or containers must be carefully labelled, well stoppered, and kept out of the way of children. If you do spill acid on to yourself or your clothing, wash with plenty of clean water and then with water and bicarbonate of soda which is an alkali which will neutralise the acid. When diluting acid, *always* add acid to the water and not vice versa.

Hydrochloric acid. Also known as spirits of salt. Don't let it get near stainless steel or other metals, except under control, for it will etch the metals. Nor should it touch nylon or any man-made fibres.

Acetic acid. Is the acid constituent of vinegar.

Oxalic acid. A poisonous acid which has many uses as a stain remover. In five per cent solution it will remove ink stains. Two teaspoonfuls of crystals in two pints of cold water will remove blood stains. In saturated solution it will remove black water marks on wood.

Citric acid. A ten per cent solution is sometimes used for stain removing.

Nitric acid. This is a strong fuming acid and if you get any on your skin it will burn severely. Any slightest amount spilt should immediately be flushed and flooded with water. Skin should be held under a running cold tap. Very diluted, it is used for cleaning gilt and gilding. It can be used to darken soft soldering.

Oleic. Acid in an oily base.

Muriatic acid. Another name for hydrochloric acid.

Accumulator acid. Diluted sulphuric acid used in the making of chlorine gas for bleaching.

ADHESIVES

The problems of getting one thing to stick to another have always loomed large for the restorer, especially when the two objects are not made of the same material. Luckily, new types of adhesive have been invented which will literally stick anything to anything. The strength of the stuck joints is also very important, and modern adhesives are so efficient that stuck joins can actually be stronger than any other kind of join, and where, in the old days the glueing of joins of all kinds was used in conjunction with other fixing methods, dowelling etc., sticking alone is nowadays often sufficiently strong. Adhesives have become so strong as well as water and heat resistant, that it is really no longer necessary to rivet ceramics, and almost totally invisible stuck joints can be made in china. Adhesives mixed with colouring matters, pigments and powders, are used as fillers, thus becoming dual purpose materials (see under *Cements and Fillers*). Most modern adhesives have many uses and will stick a very wide variety of substances, but some are better than others for particular kinds of work.

Why things stick together is quite involved and difficult to explain. Theoretically, if you can bring two surfaces together so that they touch all over their surfaces, they may stick together without adhesives. Two sheets of glass will sometimes adhere in this way and become extremely difficult to part. Even two sheets of shiny paper will stick together. I know a trick with a penny, which consists of drawing a coin sharply down a varnished wall surface, and snapping it on with a thumb. The coin will stay there indefinitely if the wall surface is all right. I suppose most of the air is expelled from under the coin, and the rim makes a perfect seal with the varnished surface, and the outside air pressure keeps the coin in place. There was a pub in Potter Heigham in Norfolk, called the Falgate, where the whole surface of the bar surround was covered in coins put there in this way. In fact my father put up the first one. Much later they were all varnished in to preserve them, but eventually the bars in the pub were enlarged and down came the panelling and the pennies. Yet few people would believe that no adhesive was used to keep the pennies up and many of the coins were there for years.

It seems that the function of an adhesive is to make the respective surfaces so smooth that they adhere. When using normal adhesives, as little as is consistent with covering the whole surface should be used, as too much just keeps the surfaces apart, and does not join them together. The join should then be put under pressure and left undisturbed.

All surfaces which are to be stuck together must first be thoroughly cleaned of old grease and glue, or rust, and the adhesive makers' instructions should be followed carefully. Glues made from gelatine or old type animal glues, can be removed by soaking with warm water. Resinous cements are dissolved by alcohol, celluloid cements can be removed with amyl acetate or acetone. Dissolvex will shift modern epoxy resin glues. Once the surfaces are cleaned they should have a rub with sand or emery paper, to make sure all glue is gone, and to give a key for the cement.

Scotch glue. Scotch glue has always been the traditional glue to use for woodwork, and it is still the best glue for veneer work especially where the veneer has to be smoothed or 'hammered' into place with the rounded end of a ball-peen hammer. Scotch glue can be bought either in cake, pearl or powder form. The glue is put into a proper glue pot with water, and left to soak overnight, which makes it swell up and soften. The glue pot is in fact two pots, one within the other. The outside one holds water, the inside one the glue, just like a double saucepan. The pot is put on to simmer and the glue stirred frequently as it heats. Don't ever boil glue, just get it hot enough to run off the brush when you hold it over the pot, without forming tears. Scotch glue is used hot and is brushed well into the surfaces. It helps to warm the wood before applying the glue. All joints made with Scotch glue should be well cramped or weighted, so that any surplus is squeezed out, and the surfaces brought as close together as possible. Scotch glue is useless for joints or mends which will be exposed to damp, as it will not hold, and in time will even grow fungus. Santobrite can be added to Scotch glue to prevent the formation of fungus. Heat also melts Scotch glue and releases joints.

Durofix. Durofix is a celluloid cement, and is extremely useful as it is transparent, so that it can be built up in layers to form a self-supporting film to repair glass etc. (although acrylic resins have supplanted it for large-scale jobs of this kind). Glass repaired with Durofix won't stand domestic handling, but for ornamental use it is good enough. One big advantage of Durofix is that it is a one tube adhesive and does not have to be mixed with hardeners.

Evo-stik. Made in several different types, this is a splendid impact adhesive. Evo-stik Impact Household Adhesive is excellent for joins where the two surfaces may be brought directly together and left without movement until set. Where joins have to be slid together (such as a mortice and tenon joint), this adhesive is not suitable. When using Evo-stik, a coat of the stuff is put on each surface to be joined, and is left for at least a quarter of an hour. The surfaces are then brought together correctly (no sliding about to get things right), and an immediate bond is made which in time is extremely strong. In fact if you try to break the bond, you may break the wood instead.

Cascamite is a powder glue which is mixed with water, is good for woodwork, as is

Aerolite which is a powder and a liquid hardener, mixed together in the right proportions for a very strong resin adhesive.

This brings me to the modern epoxy resin two-tube adhesives which are fantastically useful and versatile. There are quite a few makes, and it is not possible to list more than one or two of all the adhesives available in this section, but I think I have mentioned enough to cope with most jobs.

Plastic Padding. This is a two-tube adhesive and filler, which has a silver metallic colour. It has the advantage of drying very quickly—in ten or fifteen minutes—so that it is useful where speed is helpful. It will stick pretty well anything to anything, but its silver colour precludes its use where the join will show, or will not be painted over.

Araldite. In the two-tube pack (A.V. 100 and H.V. 100), Araldite is suitable for joining any of the materials listed below. All objects to be glued should first be cleaned, the surfaces being thoroughly degreased, then abraded, then degreased again before the adhesive is applied. Also it is important to make sure that surfaces are dry before adhesive is applied, so give them a few minutes in front of a fan heater or on a radiator; or put large objects in an airing cupboard for a while. If there is any paint or old glue on a surface to be joined, it must be removed with a solvent. Dissolvex will remove Araldite if it has been used before.

Mix your adhesive on a small piece of glass with a palette knife. Keep some methylated spirit handy for cleaning up, as it will dissolve Araldite while it is still soft. It is important that the contents of the tubes never mix except as and when you want them.

When using two-tube Araldite A.V. 100 and H.V. 100, warm the two tubes a little before measuring out and mixing the adhesive and it will be thinner, and thus easier to use, but may take a little longer to set.

For china repair Araldite A.Y. 103 and Hardener H.Y. 951 are very suitable because the mixture is thinner; it grips very hard and doesn't need much pressure to get a good join. Because it is thinner it can be got into small cracks, and it fills all the requirements of unobtrusive adhesion. It is not quite so resistant to water and steam as the two-tube Araldite, so should not be used for repairs to china which is going into domestic use.

All adhesives mixed should be used within an hour as it begins to dry after that time and gets tacky. It is sensible to have a sticking session—collecting together and preparing all the mending jobs you have on hand to do at the same time. It is quite difficult to mix the exact small amount you need for one article and only too often the whole family searches the house for things to mend to use up the adhesive. Left over mixed Araldite will keep in the freezing compartment of your refrigerator for several hours, even overnight, but do not try to keep it there indefinitely or you will end up throwing a useless little hard lump into the dustbin together with the container or sheet of glass to which it has become firmly stuck.

It is quite simple to measure out the two-tube Araldite exactly because you can squeeze an equal length strip from each tube on to the glass. With the thinner types, measurement is by drops, or even with two hypodermic syringes—although this would seem to be an expensive way of doing the job. Perhaps it is worth the investment if you are specialising in repairing things with Araldite!

Having mixed the adhesive, spread an even thin coat on each surface of the object, using a match or a rust free nail or a glass rod, and fit the two firmly together. Use gum strip to bind together a join while it dries (see section on *China*). Araldite takes twelve hours to set at room temperature, and three days to harden to maximum strength, but drying can be speeded up by heating, even by baking in a cool oven.

Drying time at	149 deg. C. (300 deg. F.)	30 mins.
	121 deg. C. (250 deg. F.)	1 hour
	79 deg. C. (175 deg. F.)	3 hours

Do not dry at over 300 deg. F. as at that heat the two-tube Araldite resin darkens.

To join the following materials (all must be degreased before and after abrasion):

Brass: Abrade with emery
Ceramics and Porcelain: Abrade with carborundum and water slurry
Copper: Abrade with emery
Glass: Abrade with carborundum
Gold: Abrade with fine emery or crocus paper
Lead, Tin and Solder: Abrade with fine emery
Leather: Degrease with great care. Abrade with glass paper
Silver: Abrade with fine emery
Steel and Iron: Abrade with emery
Stone: Abrade with a wire brush
Wood: Abrade with glasspaper

Pastes. Special pastes such as Gripfix, and photographic mounting pastes are most useful for paper work as they do not cause cockling or staining. Some photographic mountants have first to be painted on with a soft brush, and then, when the paste has dried for some minutes, the picture or paper is ironed on to its mount with a warm iron over greaseproof paper.

Paste for paper and leather similar to paperhanger's paste, proprietary brands of which can be bought, are made up as follows:

Recipe 1. ¼ lb. plain flour
½ oz. powdered alum

Mix with water to a cream, and then add a pint of cold water and heat in an enamel saucepan stirring all the time.

When using this paste for leather add a little thin Scotch glue. Keep this paste away from metal before use or it may pick up discolouring stains.

Recipe 2. 1 teaspoonful plain flour
2 teaspoonfuls cornflour
½ teaspoonful alum
3 oz. water

Mix all ingredients together well so that there are no lumps, bring to the boil in an enamel saucepan, stirring all the time, and boil for a minute or two till thick.

Copydex is an extremely useful white, rubber-based adhesive for all fabrics.

H.M.G. This heat and waterproof adhesive is good for some jobs because it is clear and quick drying, but it is not over strong. It can be handled for up to an hour, and goes totally hard in twenty-four hours. It does not slip, and is dissolved by acetone.

AMMONIA

Ammonia is a gaseous compound of nitrogen and hydrogen. It has the property in liquid form of turning grease into a soluble soap and so removing it. Used as a ten per cent solution in water it gets rid of dirt and grease, and some kinds of silver tarnish. It also makes glass and porcelain sparkle. It should never be used on bronze, and can lift varnish on wood. It is in fact, in a strong solution, quite a good varnish stripper (see *Stripping*).

Scrubbs Cloudy Ammonia is a ten per cent solution.

Ammonia solution is used for cleaning Ormolu (see *Ormolu*) and in a very dilute form, marble. A few drops added to beeswax and turpentine (see *Beeswax*) makes effective furniture polish.

ANTLERS

Antlers and horns, mounted on shaped boards—relics of our big-game-hunting grandfathers—are quite common junk objects. If it so happens that you do wish to restore such an object, clean the horns as suggested under *Ivory and Bone*. Fill any holes or chips with epoxy resin suitably coloured with kaolin powder and a little yellow ochre or brown dry powder pigment to match. Stick broken pieces back in place with Araldite, and put a wire core or pin in hollow broken horns, packed round with filler as described in the section on *China Mending*. The clean horns or antlers should be coated with a light wax polish to improve their looks. The backboard may need mending or completely stripping off, and repolishing.

Antlers which come complete with the deer's head are more difficult to cope with if the head is in bad condition. A good brushing with Fullers Earth should clean the hair, but the repair of rotted or torn leather sections may be very tricky and take careful needlework. It may be necessary to re-stuff parts of the head. A good mothproofing is always advisable, so spray well with an aerosol mothproofer, and an insecticide as well, if necessary.

ARMS AND ARMOUR

Guns and Pistols

Old firearms are popular collector's items, and no olde oake beame type of pub or café worth its salt feels fully decorated without weapons on its walls, so good ones are expensive; nevertheless one sometimes comes across old guns and pistols in junk shops and these can be in pretty bad condition. It is usually possible to mend and clean these things and make them look very decorative; by spending money they can be restored to near perfection, and you can even fire them if you dare. For really careful restoration, try to find a picture of a gun like yours or a similar actual weapon in a museum, which you can copy.

As a first step make sure that any gun you buy is not loaded. It is not ridiculous to suggest that an old pistol which has been knocking about for years could be loaded, for it has happened, and even ancient gunpowder will explode violently. Gently insert a wooden rod or dowel into the muzzle and when it will go no further make a pencil mark. Withdraw the rod and lay it alongside the barrel with the pencil mark by the muzzle and the point at which the barrel is blocked can be exactly gauged. The powder must be carefully removed. If you have a shotgun the cleaning rod which goes with it will probably have a cap on the end which unscrews to reveal a screw tip. Screw this gently into the charge in the old gun and remove it like a cork. Failing a cleaning rod, an ordinary screw welded to a piece of stiff wire would do just as well. After this the barrel should be washed out with warm water and thoroughly dried.

Unless the gun is really terribly rusted, or contrariwise is in excellent condition, it is probably best to strip it down into its component parts, just as one would when cleaning a modern gun. Normally the lock is removed first by unscrewing it from the stock. First remove the screw which holds the cock (in the flintlock) or hammer (in the percussion lock) and slide off the part. Next unscrew the pivot of the pan cover and the pan cover spring screw and remove the parts. Then unscrew the holding bolts or screws until the lock plates can be removed. (See Fig. 1.)

Penetrating oil applied to the screws and left for a while will allow many a stubborn screw to be removed. Do use well-fitting screwdrivers, as if you spoil a screw head by using a wrongly fitting screwdriver it may be impossible to get it out without drilling. The drilling out of screws is extremely tricky and may result in damage to the pistol, so don't try it unless you must. Expert help may be necessary. One way to loosen obstinate screws is first to place a little lubricating oil round the head of the screw, and then to touch the head of the screw for a second or two with the tip of a red-hot poker. This heat causes expansion and contraction to loosen the screw and the oil will penetrate and help with the withdrawal.

Dismantling a flintlock and reassembling (see Fig. 1). In order to take the lock to pieces for cleaning or repair the four screws which hold the mainspring, the sear, the sear spring and the bridle, must be half loosened. Then take out the mainspring screw and remove the mainspring. There is a pin at the rear end of the mainspring which engages in the lock plate, and the other end of the mainspring which engages in the toe of the tumbler. Compress the mainspring and it will come away easily. A hand vice is a useful tool for this job. Once the mainspring is off, the other screws may be removed and the other parts will come off quite easily.

Having cleaned all parts with fine files and emery paper or powder, and got rid of all the rust, oil everything well, and cover with Vaseline. Then set about reassembling. Fit the tumbler with its square arbour passing right through the

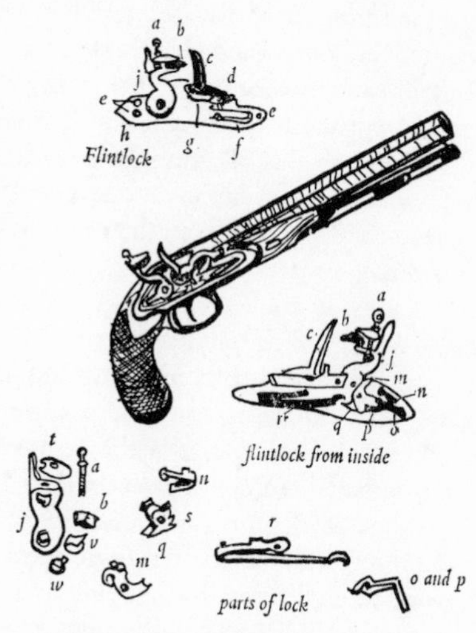

Fig. 1
FLINTLOCK DUELLING PISTOL
showing details of the lock

KEY

a set screw
b flint
c hammer
d pancover
e lock plate
retaining bolt
spring
g pan
h lock plate
cock

m bridle
n sear spring
o trigger bar
p sear
q tumbler
r mainspring
s bents
t jaw
v leather grip
w cock screw

lock plate to take the cock on the outside. The sear and the sear spring come next and then the bridle. The square lug on the sear spring fits a slot in the lock plate and holds the spring in position. Compress the mainspring and put it on the lock plate with the holding pin in position, and put the lower end of the spring back over the tumbler toe. Then secure the screw. Without a hand vice, depress the tumbler to the fired position so that the end of the mainspring will go over it. Then put the cock on and pull it back to the half cocked position so that the tumbler toe comes and compresses the mainspring. The rest of the pieces are put back in the reverse order to removal, the pan cover spring and pan cover going on last.

The barrel of the gun comes off next. This has a metal extension called a tang which runs into the stock. The tang screws are removed, and any retaining bands or pins. Trigger guard, butt cap and ramrod pipes are usually screwed or pinned in place and must be removed with care. If a gun is in bad condition it is likely that the rusty screws and pins are stuck into the wooden stock parts, and too much beef will merely result in breaking off chunks of wood complete with the pins and screws. Gentle tapping and the judicious use of penetrating oil will help. But leave things where they are rather than risk breaking the stock. Expert gunsmiths make their own castings and spare parts, but for those without the necessary tools or ability, castings can be bought, which only need filing to fit. Normans of Framlingham in Suffolk specialise in these parts and have a comprehensive catalogue.

Guns will be more or less rusty, either with ordinary brown rust or that black rust which seems to have eaten right into the metal and looks like black ink stains. When restoring or cleaning any kind of metal, the rule is not to overdo things. Gentle abrasives, gentle cleaners and gentle fingers give the best results. Patience is better than a power tool. Start by applying a mixture of oil and paraffin, or by soaking the metal parts in it. Patent rust removers are fine if used with care. They should never be left on for a very long time, or they will etch the metal, and will probably dull it, although in this case can always be re-polished. Penetrating oil contains rust remover, so if you have been using this to remove screws, be sure to wipe it all off the metal before leaving the work for any length of time. Clean the inside of the barrel with a wire brush on a rod.

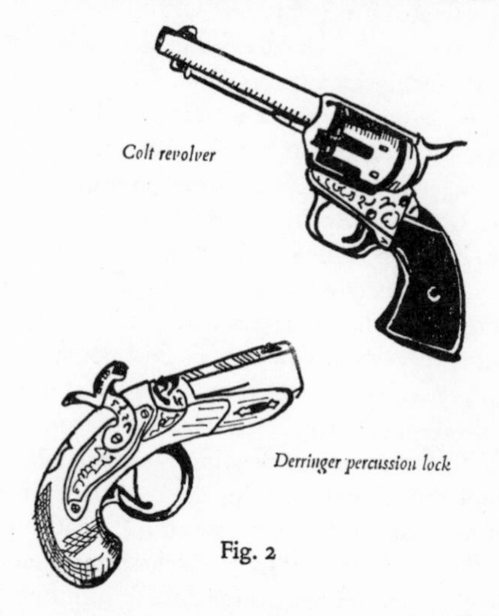

Fig. 2

Having cleaned off all possible rust, polish the metal work with jeweller's emery, which is considerably finer than ordinary emery paper and comes in various grades (see *Abrasives*). Start with a coarse grade and finish with fine grades and you can get a mirror finish. Don't be too quick to resort to buffing wheels or harsh abrasives; you may make deep scratches or rub off marks or chasings which cannot be replaced. Barrels may have a brown colour which is due to deliberate rusting, so that the barrel would not rust further while the gun was in use. To re-brown a barrel it must first be polished mirror bright and then treated with many successive solutions of a certain acid formula. Gunsmiths guard these formulae closely, and most send their barrels to an acknowledged expert to have the job done. It costs several pounds and would probably not be worth your while, simply to restore a not very valuable piece of junk.

Blue barrels were originally coloured by a heat process. Blueing is equally an expert's job which takes time and experience, although solutions can be bought which enable the amateur to blue barrels quite effectively.

Clean brass parts, trigger guards, ramrod pipes, butt caps, etc. with ordinary metal polish. If these are missing new ones can be bought (see above) and fitted by filing.

Having achieved the polish and colour you want, the next thing is to maintain it. Be very careful not to handle the metal parts of your gun after its final polish, as sweaty fingers leave a deposit which causes spots of rust. (This applies to all metal work.) A piece of wood carefully jammed in the muzzle will make a temporary handle while applying a final finish to the gun. Wipe over the metal parts with a very thin layer of oil; or if you don't like this, try wiping with a duster which is impregnated with silicone—these can be bought for dusting furniture in any hardware store. Some people like to lacquer things on the principle that lacquering reduces cleaning to a minimum. Unless lacquer is of extremely good quality, it will darken in time and altogether spoil the look of the job. (See *Lacquer*.)

The wooden stocks or butts are another matter, and often need a lot of repair. The stock may be completely split.

Modern impact adhesives, such as Evo-stik, make a strong join very easy, but it is best to make sure that they do fit accurately, as with impact adhesives once the two faces of a join are put together they must remain if a good join is to be made. If the stock is chipped or if there is a piece missing, you are going to have to find a piece of more or less matching wood to replace it. Clean the old stock first with fine steel wool and linseed oil. Rub away until the dirt and any old varnish has gone, then you will be able to see the grain and colour of the wood. Finding the right piece of wood may be difficult. A friendly furniture restorer is about the most likely man to help—you will only need a small piece anyway. Whittle the new wood to fit with a sharp knife and fine sandpaper. If you are an expert wood-carver and have the tools, making a matching piece should be no problem. Remember, having bonded new and old, that it may be necessary to bore small holes for the pins or screws to take the metal parts when the pistol is reassembled and this should be done with care. When the bond is set, rub the whole stock well with linseed before reassembling the gun.

Shallow dents in wooden gun stocks can sometimes be reduced by steaming. Soak a piece of thick cloth in hot water and put it over the dent and then hold a hot iron on the cloth and get up a good head of steam; this swells the wood and reduces the dents a little, but as the wood dries right out they will probably reappear to some degree.

Gunstocks are often attacked by woodworm and if this has happened, treat the stock with an anti-woodworm dressing such as Rentokil. If the stock is badly honey-combed, inject synthetic resin into the holes with a hypodermic syringe or even soak it in a thin mix to stiffen the whole thing.

Burr walnut (see *Woods*) is most commonly used for

gun stocks and is mainly imported. You would probably have to buy a new stock blank through the trade and shape it to fit, if a whole new stock is required.

Of course if you can get hold of several pistols all more or less alike, you can make up composite restorations using sound parts from each. What you will have at the finish is a fake, not a restoration, but if it is just for decoration, then it doesn't really matter, and only an expert will be able to tell that it isn't the genuine article!

The periodical *Guns Review* contains much interesting information about antique firearms.

Swords

Swords turn up in junk shops in odd lots with old hickory shafted golf clubs, broken walking sticks and elderly umbrellas, and are usually a relic of somebody's great grandfather's service in the cavalry. The services still use dress swords and ceremonial swords, and these, being expensive items, get handed on and do not appear in junk shops. Valuable old swords are real collector's items and you are unlikely to be trying to restore one of these. However, any old sword can look quite fine once it has been cleaned and polished. Knives and daggers and bayonets come into the same category and are perhaps more common in junk shops. Very often the scabbard, particularly if it is an Oriental one, is as attractive as the weapon itself and warrants as much care as the blade.

As with the restoration and cleaning of any kind of metal object, care is needed. Too violent attempts at rust removal may remove interesting marks or engraving or inlay, and half the fun of cleaning up these things is in what may come to light underneath.

A sword, like a gun, can be dismantled into its component parts, and if this can be done without breaking the weapon or damaging it, it is far better to take it apart for cleaning. Blades were often made somewhere other than the hilts or sheaths, and the whole assembled by swordsmiths before sale. Parts got broken and were replaced, and a sword or a dagger can be a composite bearing different makers' marks and still be quite genuine. If you find a sheathed sword in a junk shop, take it carefully out of the sheath holding the whole thing pointed downward. Be especially careful with knives and daggers for an old scabbard can split as you take out the weapon which may still be razor sharp.

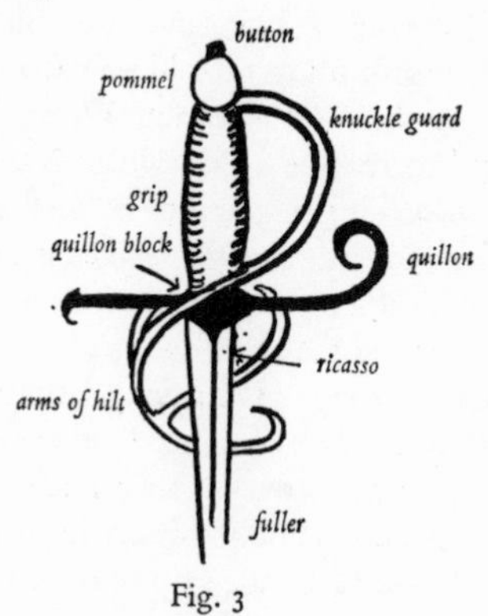

Fig. 3

To take a sword apart (see Fig. 3) first check the button at the top of the hilt. The tang, or top end of the blade, passes right up through the hilt and the pommel at the top, and is then burred over the button to hold the whole thing together. File off the overlap and slide the blade from the hilt; but it may not come out that easily. Later swords may have a screw-in button. Grip the blade in a vice, near the top, but make sure the vice is padded, or the sword well wrapped, so that it will not be marked by the vice.

Using a piece of hard wood as a punch, tap the base of the pommel upwards away from the grip, working round and round it till it loosens and the hilt begins to slide off the blade; but do be careful not to damage anything. Best leave well alone if there is no movement at all. Penetrating oil may help, if you can get some to run between the tang of the blade and the hilt. If the sword has only a small pommel, tap the hilt round the shells, at the bottom. Once again, be very careful for it is terribly easy to break castings.

Now the blade and the hilt are separate and can be coped with on their merits. If the grip is wooden and covered with leather, it may be split, and you will have to carve yourself a new grip using the old one as a pattern. Beech and walnut are the most common woods, but any wood could be used to remake a grip which is to be covered—after all the sword is not going to be used in battle. If the grip is leather-covered, and the leather is sound, give it a good dose of leather dressing. There are various proprietary dressings and the same one can be used on a leather sheath. Some dressings give a long-lasting finish, others need more frequent renewing (see *Leather Dressings*).

A new leather grip cover can be made quite easily by cutting out a piece from any suitable leather. Clean off all the old leather and make the grip smooth and clean. Then very carefully pare or bevel the edges of the new leather grip so that they fit round the handle without a ridge where the join comes. Soak the leather and put it on the grip, smoothing it to fit. Then bind it on to dry. Rubber bands may leave grooves in the leather, so some kind of wide tape or bandage just to hold it in position while it dries is better. When the leather is quite dry, remove the binding, and, very carefully, the leather piece which should by now be exactly the right shape and fit. Using an adhesive, such as Evo-stik which will not stain the leather, stick it firmly to the wooden grip. Very often hilts are wholly or partly bound with brass wire. If this has to be replaced, two strands of brass piano wire or picture wire, twisted together, make a good job. The actual binding is not so easy as the ends of the wire have to be neatly tucked in.

The cleaning of metal hilts and blades must be carefully done. Brass and silver hilts will probably come up well with ordinary metal polishes and some elbow grease, but steel hilts will need rubbing with abrasive. Make up various pads and sticks to help with the rubbing down, checking that the stick is well padded with foam rubber under the emery paper; this makes it easier to get into difficult corners. Blades which have inlay should be treated very gently, as any rough treatment will bring it off. Soap and water and a soft cloth for drying are the best; certainly it is dangerous to use strong metal polishes or rust removing preparations. Clean plain blades and steel hilts with oil and paraffin mixture to remove loose rust, and then wash with strong detergent to get rid of all grease. Clean very greasy metal with carbon tetrachloride. Then wipe rust remover on the metal and remove it after a few minutes. You will get some idea of how much rust is going to shift, and can repeat the treatment until the metal is clean. The big danger is that rust remover, if left too long, will work unevenly and will start to etch the metal, and you will end up with a pitted surface. Oriental swords are very often meant to have a dull finish, and after a wipe over with rust remover, all they will need is a polish with a soft cloth, whereas Western steel is worked over with emery until it has a mirror finish. Don't get fingerprints on to the polished metal or they will form rust spots in time. Rub the finished metal over with a light film of oil, or use a silicone-impregnated duster or silicone furniture polish, sparingly, on a soft cloth. Lacquer, if used, must be of high quality, or it will darken in time and have to be removed. Lacquer is really a lazy and not wholly satisfactory way of finishing polished metals (see *Lacquer*).

If metal parts of the hilt, quillons, shell guards etc., are broken or damaged, it may be possible to braze carefully shaped new parts into place, but this does seem to me to be a job for the expert as it requires special tools and a knowledge of technique.

If the top of the tang was filed off to free the blade, hammer out the tang a little so that there is something to burr over again on replacement. Be very careful, and hammer gently with the tang laid flat on a block. Reassemble hilt and blade and tap it into position tapping the pommel well home. Use a small mallet or a piece of wood, not a metal hammer. Burr over the top of the tang with a punch and file it smooth and neat.

If your sword or dagger has a metal scabbard, treat it in the same way as the blade, cleaning with great care if it has any engraving or inlay. If it is plain, wipe it with rust remover and rub with abrasive, and finish it with a silicone wipe.

Damaged leather scabbards take some mending. If the stitching has gone, it may be possible to restitch it, but often the holes have broken out and the leather is dry and dead anyway and won't hold stitches. Just stick the edges together as neatly as you can with adhesive.

If the scabbard is broken, insert a strip of cardboard or veneer or plastic to support it. If leather is in good condition all it needs is a wipe with ordinary leather dressing. Some scabbards have been stained and polished or boned, these are best retouched and polished with ordinary leather polish.

Armour

Old pieces of armour, even complete suits picked up in very bad condition, can be completely cleaned and done up. The methods used for cleaning sword blades, guns etc. are suitable for armour. Museums use a phosphoric acid cleaner known as Deoxidine.

I know of someone who bought a terribly rusty old suit of armour for £20, without knowing anything about it, and cleaned and restored it and sold it for £300. I suppose the basic cost of £20 puts it outside the category of junk, but it is the kind of profit one likes to dream about.

Burnishing. Any cavalry man will tell you that the only way to get swords, cuirasses, spurs, bits irons etc. chromium bright is to burnish them. They are first cleaned with metal polish and then burnished. A burnisher is a leather pad with small steel rings like chain mail sewn to it, and the object to be burnished is rubbed very hard with this pad. The metal will come to chromium brightness if you use enough elbow grease. The object is then greased very lightly, or lacquered to preserve the shine; but before doing this, small objects can be kept dry and bright in a bag of bran.

By the way, the shoulder pieces of a trooper's dress uniform, which look like pieces of chain mail, are in fact ornamental burnishers.

Bits, irons and spurs are ornamental enough to become collectors' items, and they should be burnished as described, or by being put into a canvas bag with a handful of ball-bearings and swung around for a bit. It is an old trick to burnish a curb chain by folding it inside a big duster or piece of cloth, and then, holding both ends tightly, to swing it about with a circular motion.

BAMBOO FURNITURE

Bamboo furniture (hall stands, tables etc.) is rather rickety, and repairing it is rather a matter of careful glueing and dowelling. When a piece of bamboo has been badly broken it will probably be a splintery split rather than a clean break. A wooden rod or dowel inserted through the middle of the bamboo will strengthen it so that you can tidy up the break and stick the splinters down again (see Fig. 4). The hollow bamboo is blocked at each ring and a hole will have to be bored right through so that the dowel can pass along. If you don't possess a long enough bit, a red-hot iron or steel rod will burn a hole through, but be careful not to set the whole thing alight.

If the splintering is so bad that a lot of it has to be removed, the piece can be built up again with Araldite suitably coloured, either yellow ochre or mottled brown. A good cleansing furniture polish will bring up the bamboo to a good shine, but epoxy resins don't polish well. If you

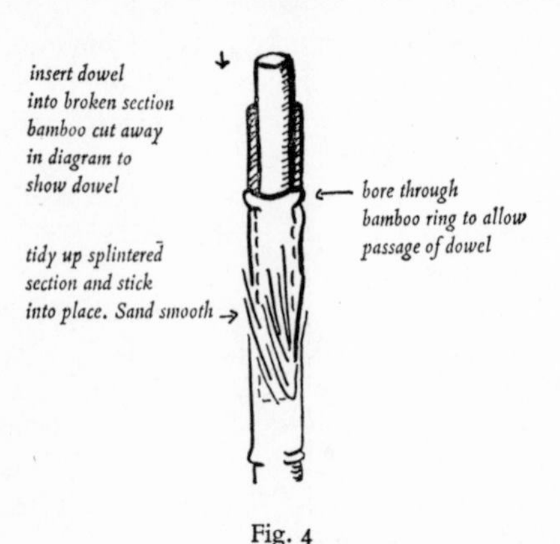

Fig. 4

want a permanent waterproof finish, clean off the bamboo thoroughly with a solvent to remove any old wax or polish; then wash and dry it and paint or spray the bamboo with polyurethane varnish or glaze such as Ronseal Hardglase or Translac.

BAROMETERS

If a barometer needs to be repaired, it is best to take it to an instrument repairer, but the cases themselves were often beautifully made, and quite worth using for some other purpose. The case of an aneroid barometer with the works removed might make a good frame for a small mirror, or, filled in with a suitable piece of wood, a base for any kind of object, such as a ship model.

BASKET WORK, CANEWORK, WICKERWORK, RUSHWORK

All kinds of furniture incorporating these materials turn up in junk shops. They are often in quite reasonable condition except for the grime of years ingrained in all the cracks and crevices, and for discolouration and fading.

Deal with the stuff in the garden on a warm sunny day by washing it very thoroughly with soap and warm water on cotton wool or a soft rag. Then dry it well and leave it in the sun for several hours, and the sunlight will bleach the basket work. Wickerwork chairs won't hurt by being lightly scrubbed with cold salt water and will bleach quite a bit in the sun. Very dilute domestic bleach will whiten these materials without damage.

Stick together any pieces which have become unravelled with Evo-stik, and the following day, polish the chair with a silicone furniture polish or cream. To make a semi-permanent protective skin apply a thin solution of acrylic resin such as Technovit, or a clear polyurethane glaze. These coatings will prevent dirt from getting at the wicker again, and will bind any pieces which tend to split or flake apart. The surface will be glossy, but because it is broken won't have the over-bright mirror effect that these glazes give to plain wood.

To preserve wickerwork without glazing it, apply a paint of white beeswax dissolved in benzene (see *Beeswax*).

BATTERSEA ENAMELS

Genuine Battersea boxes, snuff boxes, trinket boxes etc. are rare, and are made of copper surfaced with opaque glass decorated by hand painting or by transfer painting. Any kind of small decorated box which turns up in a junk shop is liable to be labelled Battersea, and probably isn't. As to cleaning and repairing such items, a wipe with a squeezed-out soap swab, a thorough drying, and then a rub over with Renaissance wax should do the trick. Don't use solvents in case non-synthetic glues have been used.

BEADWORK

Beadwork was once quite a popular art, and 19th-century young ladies seemed to have spent a lot of time at it, making purses, book covers, tea cosies and even ambitious things like screens. A wash in warm soapy water is about the best way to clean it, but dry it immediately and carefully in case there are any metallic beads which might rust. Repairs are a matter of good needlework. Some of the beads won't pass a needle; in this case use nylon thread which can be pushed through. To stiffen the tip of the piece of thread, dip it in a little melted candle grease and roll it between your fingers.

BEDROOM CHINA

There is still quite a lot of this about and it's quite pretty. The most obvious use for old chamber pots, slop pails, washbasins, foot baths, ewers, etc. is for flowers, or to hold flower pots. This china has been used for soup tureens, punch bowls etc. and provided there are no cracks or chips in the china, I suppose there is no reason why not, but personally the idea does not appeal. Like other pottery it can be mended (see *China Mending*), and a bit of careful re-touching with a paint brush and enamel can brighten things up a bit.

BEESWAX

Beeswax is the natural wax made by the bees when building honeycombs, and it can be bought at chemists and some hardware stores. It is sold as fine grade, white beeswax, or as natural wax which has an orange brown colour. Of course if you keep bees you will have your own. I once left a bowl of natural beeswax from my own bees on a larder shelf. In due course, at a moment of family crisis, a visitor tried to fry some bacon and eggs in it, mistaking it for dripping. The kitchen smelt wonderful for days, but otherwise it was a waste not only of the beeswax, but of the bacon and eggs!

Beeswax by itself is too hard to use as a polish, and various blends can be made. Beeswax melts at about 65 deg. C. and do take care when making polish as the ingredients are inflammable. Keep an old saucepan for the job and have suitable containers with good lids ready for the polish. I keep my old furniture polish tins and re-use them again and again. Use real turpentine, *not* turpentine substitute.

Recipe 1. 3 parts white beeswax
8 parts real turpentine

Melt the wax slowly over a low flame, together with the turpentine. Use a double saucepan if possible, or suspend the container in another saucepan with water in it. Colour the polish with stain if you wish. The stain should be added immediately the concoction is removed from the heat, and mixed in well. Put the polish into a tin and close it tightly. Use it just like any other polish when cold; apply with a soft rag and rub hard.

Recipe 2. ½ lb. beeswax
real turpentine

Melt the wax in a saucepan over a low flame, adding turpentine and mixing well until the whole is the consistency of thick custard. Paint the mixture on to the wood with a rag while it is still warm and leave it to dry. Then polish as hard and as long as you like. This method is best for natural wood surfaces which will absorb a lot of the polish, but not for surfaces which already have a polish on them.

Recipe 3. 8 ozs. beeswax
2 ozs. resin
real turpentine

Melt the resin, beeswax and a little turpentine in a double saucepan over a low flame. When it is all blended together remove it from the heat and allow it to cool, but before it has set stir in enough turpentine to make a soft polish, about ¼ pt. Add colouring if required.

Recipe 4. This is a leather dressing similar to that used by the British Museum.
7 ozs. anhydrous lanolin
1 fluid oz. cedarwood oil
½ oz. white beeswax
11 fluid ozs. hexane

Hexane is highly inflammable so do not make this mixture up near an open flame, or use the dressing near an open flame. Dissolve the beeswax in the hexane (no heat is required), add the lanoline and blend well, and lastly add the cedarwood oil.

Recipe 5. furniture cream
3 ozs. white wax
8 ozs. real turpentine
8 ozs. warm water
liquid ammonia

Melt the white wax over a low flame. Remove the saucepan from the flame and add the turpentine and the warm water and blend it all together. Add the ammonia drop by drop stirring all the time until the mixture is a thick cream. This old recipe for polish should be used with care as ammonia is a solvent for some varnishes but is excellent on wood which does not have an artificial surface of varnish or French polish.

Recipe 6. ½ pt. real turpentine
½ pt. soft water
2 ozs. beeswax (natural)
1 oz. white wax
2 squares camphor
1 oz. Castile soap
1 teaspoonful ammonia

Shred the waxes and the camphor into the turpentine. Shred the soap into the water and simmer until the volume is reduced by half. Cool and add the turpentine and wax mixture. Blend well together and add the ammonia and shake thoroughly. This is a good cleansing furniture polish.

Recipe 7. 2 ozs. white beeswax
benzene

Flake the beeswax and then add the benzene and stir until the wax has dissolved. This is a useful dressing for preserving wickerwork and cane.

Recipe 8. wax adhesive
5 parts beeswax
5 parts resin
1 part real turpentine

Heat all together gently in a double saucepan until the ingredients blend.

Simple beeswax polishes as in Recipe 1 make an excellent protective coating for bronze, alabaster, iron, steel, marble and slate, as well as for all kinds of wooden furniture and objects.

Various other polishes which do not contain wax are described in the section on *Polishes*.

BIRD-CAGES

Large Victorian bird-cages still turn up in junk shops. I owned and used one, but unfortunately my Siamese cat discovered that the metal rods were not particularly strong, and after I came home from the cinema one night to find a pathetic heap of blue feathers on the floor, a smug cat, and a bent cage, I reverted to modern steel cages and kept the old one as a relic. Many old cages are somehow reminiscent of the Crystal Palace, and are made of dozens of metal rods, either rusted or covered in filth and old paint. The only real answer is to clean each rod separately with emery paper, or steel wool dipped in paint stripper. It's hard work on the fingers and is a good job for the long winter evenings, as it can be done while watching television.

Solder broken rods (see *Soldering*). Having cleaned the cage repaint it, or lacquer it with clear metal lacquer. The application of paint or lacquer by brushing is a tedious job on such an object; spraying might be easier, but to be sure of covering all sides of the rods; dipping is the best answer. If the cage can be taken into sections each section should be dealt with separately, otherwise you are going to need a huge container and an awful lot of paint or lacquer to dip the object effectively.

BLEACHING

Colour or stains can be removed by bleaching. Sunlight will bleach, but it is chemical bleaching which is described in this section. Because the action of bleach is irrevocable take care. It is all too easy to remove not only the stain and the colour but the underlying material; and it is a cardinal rule to use bleach well diluted and to strengthen it gradually if necessary. Always try out bleach on a part of the material where it can do least damage, before making any general applications.

Hydrogen peroxide, and Milton are good bleaches. To bleach very fragile articles which cannot be rubbed, soak a Plaster of Paris slab with hydrogen peroxide and then place the object to be bleached just above the slab, within a quarter of an inch. Do this in an empty drawer or a small cupboard to confine and concentrate the vapours.

Household bleaches such as Domestos, Brobat, and Parazone are fine for bleaching certain articles, but are strong and may need dilution and they should not be mixed with any other type of cleaner lest you succeed in making chlorine gas which is highly toxic.

Chloromine T, which is white powder to mix with distilled water, makes a bleach for prints.

Raw wood is bleached, either after stripping down or to remove stains, by swabbing with ordinary domestic bleach. Adjust the strength of the solution according to the degree of lightness required.

Recipe 1. bleach for fox marks or small spots on paper
1 oz. chloride of lime (calcium oxychloride)
1 gallon of distilled water
4 fluid ozs. pure hydrochloric acid
1 gallon of distilled water

Make a separate bath in each gallon of water with each chemical.

Recipe 2. bleaching paste for ivory
whiting
20 volume hydrogen peroxide

Make a stiff paste.

Recipe 3. bath for textiles
1 part of hydrogen peroxide
20 parts cold water

Bleaching Box. Chlorine gas is a highly poisonous gas, which has an affinity with hydrogen. It will unite with the hydrogen in water, freeing the oxygen, and this means that it has strong bleaching properties. It is possible to make an apparatus for bleaching prints etc., but I must point out that chlorine gas is dangerous stuff and the greatest care should be taken when using it as a bleach, and all children and animals should be miles away.

The first necessity is a flat box large enough to take the biggest prints you intend to bleach (see Fig. 5). It must be well made with airtight joints. A sheet of thick glass should be used as a lid, for it enables you to see what is going on, and it must fit the top of the box snugly. If you are doing a proper job, make a frame top and hinge it for the box to drop in on to a narrow ledge, and putty the glass into the frame. Fix a handle to the lid so that it can be lifted up easily. Bore a hole in the side of the box and cement a piece of glass tubing to take the gas pipe. Having made your box, test it with a puff or two of cigarette smoke to make sure it is gas tight.

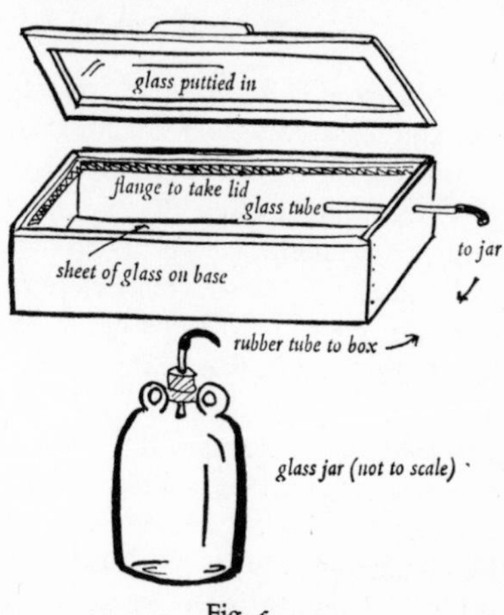

Fig. 5

Get a gallon cider jar with a well fitting rubber cork with a hole in it to take a short length of glass tube. Join the tube in the cork to the tube in the side of the box with a rubber tube. Place another sheet of glass in the bottom of the box, damp the print which is to be bleached and lay it in the box. Close the lid. Put two ounces of bleaching powder (chloride of lime) into the jar, pour in a cupful of accumulator acid, and close the jar at once. If this job can be done in the open air, all the better. If there is any leakage of gas, keep away until it has dispersed. When the print is sufficiently bleached, just open the lid and let the air blow away the gas, always being careful not to inhale.

The amount of gas which will be made by the quantities given here is not enough to give a dangerous concentration, but nevertheless it is not to be fooled with. Don't do this job in a room with birds, fish, cats, dogs or children in it. Or even white mice.

BONE AND IVORY

Small bone and ivory objects—card cases, chessmen, statuettes, fans, needles, inlays and small carvings turn up from time to time in bad condition and in need of cleaning. Impregnate really badly broken or chipped or cracked pieces with melted paraffin wax, which will hold the piece together and preserve it. Warm the object first over a radiator or in an airing cupboard, and put it right into the runny wax. Lift it out after a few minutes and wipe off the surplus.

Ivory goes yellow with age especially if it is *not* exposed to light. Sometimes this colour is pleasant and is best left alone, but things like knife handles, piano keys or fan sticks do look better white. Make up a bleaching paste of whiting and 20 volume hydrogen peroxide and coat the piece with it. The paste must be stiff or the ivory will absorb too much liquid and swell. Stand the object out in the air and sunshine until the paste has dried, then wash it off and dry the piece thoroughly with a soft cloth. A little almond oil applied with a soft rag will leave a nice protective coating.

To clean bone and ivory which just needs dirt and dust removing from crevices, use methylated spirit on a duster, or on a soft brush. Never use water. If there are spots which won't come off, try rubbing the spot with a little whiting and methylated spirit on a cotton wool swab on a cocktail stick.

Bone and ivory can be polished with tripoli, or rottenstone or carborundum products, or with silica preparations and modern metal polishes.

Stick broken pieces of ivory together with Durofix or Araldite. Make sure the surfaces to be joined are clean, and bleach out any staining left by old glue as above.

BOOKS

The top edges of books get filthy and although loose dust can be removed with a soft brush or an old fashioned feather-duster, real dirt is hard to clear. Holding the book very tightly shut it so that only the top edges show, rub gently with fine sandpaper folded to the correct size. This could be rather too fierce for a valuable book, so try soft breadcrumbs, or an art eraser (see Fig. 6).

The edges of many old books are either gilded or painted, and it is quite easy to give these a new lease of life. Ordinary water colour paint mixed with size instead of water is brushed on. The book must be well cramped with the covers folded out of the way, and the exposed pages protected, or the paint may colour more than it is meant to.

To re-gild, Restoration Wax or Treasure Wax Gilt should be rubbed on the tightly closed edges with your finger, and then polished with a soft cloth to remove the surplus and make it shine.

Leather covers on books must be cleaned occasionally with a little leather polish such as Sheerwax, but remember that on most books the leather is almost paper thin, and cannot take too much rough handling. Very often old books are quite spoiled by pieces of the leather being torn

Fig. 6

away to show the cardboard cover, or else the leather on the spine is split or perished. To mend these tears, cut out the bad parts, clean off the old glue and muck, gently lift and stick the new piece of leather into position, being careful to tuck the new edges under the old. The leather for this job should be as thin as possible, and do pare the tucked in edges carefully, so that the joins do not make a nasty bulge. For any decoration that has to be done, see the section on Leather.

Print on book titles and authors' names with Indian Ink

or Reeves Transfer Foil, which is used rather like carbon paper. You will probably find that it needs a little practice to make a neat job of the lettering, especially on the curved spine.

If a book has the side cover torn away from the spine, Sellotape X will make a strong lengthwise join, with a small gap left between the two edges, so that there is enough play left, when the book is closed. Sheets of coloured paper cut to size and pasted over the end page and the cardboard cover look neat. Seccotine or paperhanger's paste are useful adhesives for binding and paper work.

Stained and damp pages are dealt with in the same way as prints (see section on cleaning prints), but this can be rather difficult without taking the book to pieces. When the odd page is dirty or stained, particularly at the beginning or end, a little gentle dabbing with carbon tetrachloride, petrol or benzine should remove most greasy marks and fingerprints. Wax is best dealt with by placing a piece of blotting paper under the spot, and ironing lightly with a hot iron.

If a book should happen to be dropped in the bath, dry it by putting tissue paper or sheets of blotting paper between the leaves, through half the book. Then put an even weight on the book and leave it in a dry place, perhaps in the draught of a fan heater or a hair dryer, but do not put it too near a radiator or fire. The current of air is necessary to carry away moisture. Treat the second half of the book the same way when the first has dried.

Mend torn pages with white paste (see recipe under *Adhesives*), as other glues will show either too grey or brown. On frayed or ragged overlapping edges, put a little paste on one surface, and place the torn sheet exactly over it. If a corner or edge of a sheet is missing, cut another piece of paper, similar in texture and colour, slightly larger than the missing portion, and stick it on to the torn piece. A tidier job is made by trimming the torn piece first. When a page is torn across the print, mend it by sticking the thinnest possible Japanese paper over the top. If the print is large and the lines well spaced, cut little strips of matching paper, and stick them in between the print, although this is horribly fiddly. The edge of a torn page should always be reinforced so that it will not tear again in the same place. Whole pages torn out of books are best repaired with long strips of matching paper pasted down the length of the tears. Sellotape X can be used, but if there are quite a lot of pages out, it will make clumsy joins, and ordinary sellotape is not good as the edges of it stay sticky and pick up bits of dirt and dust, making a grey mark.

Insect infestation in books is dealt with under *Insects*.

BOULLE, BUHL or BOULE

A certain Frenchman called André Charles Boulle, who died in 1732, invented this work which bears his name in a variety of spellings. Wooden objects, boxes, desks, clocks etc. were covered with a combination of metal, tortoiseshell, mother of pearl, bone, ivory, brass, ebony, and sometimes silver. The work is very over-decorated but it appealed to the Victorians and continued to be made until comparatively recently.

The surface of the wood is engraved with designs in brass, the lines of the engraving being picked out with black pigment, and any part that isn't covered with inlay of one kind or another is surfaced with tortoiseshell.

Animal and fish glues were all that was available in the days when Boulle was made, so be careful not to use solvents to clean it. Take very great care when cleaning to use suitable cleaners for each part of the surface. A careful wipe with a swab of cotton wool squeezed out in mild detergent will help if the work is very dirty, but be careful not to get water under any lifted inlay.

Where inlay has been lifted, or even, in the case of metal parts, bent, straighten it very carefully and clean all the old glue off the reverse surfaces. Scrape as much old glue as possible off the bed in which the inlay lies, and replace the inlay using a synthetic glue for the job. To cut and replace lost pieces of any of the inlay is difficult and calls for real craftsmanship, and would probably be beyond the amateur. The difficulty, unless you have been stacking up odds and ends for years, is to find suitable matching pieces. Once the piece has been restored, polish the whole thing with a little Renaissance wax polish.

See also *Furniture*.

BRUSHES

A good selection of brushes should always be kept if you are restoring junk. Not only for putting things on, but for taking things off. If possible keep a different brush for each kind of paint, resin, glue, acid etc. that you use, and always clean brushes immediately after use. Having removed all traces of paint etc. hang them up to dry. Two nails banged into the wall just wide enough apart to take the handle make a good brush holder.

Apart from the large size paint brushes, smaller brushes of camel hair (usually cow hair), sable, or hogs bristle, such as those used by artists, are ideal for small retouching jobs.

For cleaning, various brushes should be kept quite dry and not used for other purposes. Keep old toothbrushes, soft and hard nail brushes, shaving brushes, soft and hard small clothes brushes; all are useful.

Metal brushes made of brass wire (sometimes used for

cleaning suede shoes) are handy, and steel wire brushes are helpful for removing rust, but are rather drastic.

If you are using a brush for paint or varnish and you want to leave the job for a while, during lunch or even overnight, and do not want to go to the trouble of cleaning it, wrap the brush in a piece of aluminium baking foil and put it in the freezing compartment of the fridge. This avoids any dilution of the paint on the brush by standing it in turpentine etc.

Lens brushes as used by photographers make extremely good brushes for dusting really fragile work.

Brushes with glass fibre hairs can be bought to use for applying acids which might attack ordinary bristles.

Cleaning brushes. Clean brushes thoroughly immediately you have finished each job. Use Polyclens to wash them first and then put them under a cold tap. Or you can clean them with solvent according to the paint you have been using. Brushes used for oil based paints, varnishes, enamels, may be suspended in paraffin or turpentine for a while, squeezed between wads of newpaper or old rags and then washed in hot soapy water. Rinse in cold water and hang up to dry. Never leave brushes with the base resting on a shelf or the bottom of a jar, or they will shape as they dry. It is better to leave them lying flat on their sides, if you cannot hang them up between two nails.

Brushes used for cellulose paint or lacquers must be washed in cellulose thinners. Rinse the brush in thinners several times, and then wash in soap and water, working up a lather on the side of the bowl, or on the palm of your hand. Then rinse the brush in warm water and put it away.

Emulsion paint and distemper wash out with water.

Clean rubber paint off with petrol.

Wash brushes used for polyurethane lacquers in turpentine substitute and then hot soapy water.

Brushes that have been allowed to get into a really bad state can be cleaned with proprietory cleaners. Use any of the appropriate chemical solvents to clean badly clogged brushes, but it may take a fair quantity and could be a little expensive. The real answer is to clean brushes as soon as they have been used, while the job is easy. Personally if a brush gets really bad I discard it and buy a new one rather than risk spoiling a job with a dirty brush. A dirty old brush is one bit of junk I never try to restore.

CHINA AND GLASS

China restoration is always delicate work, requiring care, accuracy and knowledge of technique. How much knowledge depends entirely on how ambitious you are. Most people, if they fail in simple efforts to stick china together, take it to a professional restorer if the piece is of any value. It also depends on what is going to happen to a piece after it is mended. If it is to stand peacefully on a shelf, then the repair need not be so strong as it would have to be for domestic use. Some people try to restore a piece to the state where only a very close scrutiny will reveal the mend. It is technically possible to fool even ultra violet light. Others feel that there is no shame in a few cracks in old china. Like so many skills connected with making and mending things, china restoring can develop from the ability simply to stick broken pieces together, to the most complex dowelling and pinning and moulding and modelling and casting and painting. It can start by being a chore and end by being an art, which like any art develops into pride in craftsmanship, and pleasure in achievement. Maybe the kind of painstaking repair I am thinking of comes outside the scope of a book on restoring junk, but I shall include an outline of some of the methods and materials and tools needed just in case you do decide to venture further than a little bit of glueing.

Some technical colleges run classes on china restoration, but they are few and far between, although this is one of the best ways to gain expert knowledge and experience. The study of books on the subject and plenty of practice should make you reasonably efficient if you are not totally ham-fisted!

There are so many objects in so many shapes and sizes made of so many materials; so many 'pots' that it is difficult to detail all the techniques, and each job must be treated on its merits. The first and easiest method is to mend by sticking. Sticking things together used to be more difficult than it is now, because the old adhesives were nothing like so easy to use or so heat-and-water-resistant, so free from shrinkage, or attacks by fungus, so clean, so invisible, or so strong. The invention of cellulose glues and epoxy resin adhesives has completely revolutionised sticking, and made it possible to mend things with adhesive alone where riveting, dowelling, or pinning would once have been essential.

As a general rule, a piece of china, be it a plate, a pot, a statuette, or a vase, can be mended by sticking alone if the two faces come together properly and neatly and if they can be made to stay in position while the adhesive is setting.

If a part such as a curved handle, or the limb of a figurine, is broken, perhaps in more than one place, and there are pieces missing; or if the surfaces to be joined are chipped and do not fit, or there are whole sections missing; then more ambitious methods will have to be used. Whole sections can be remade by modelling with epoxy resins just as the sculptor models, or by making plaster moulds and taking castings. Large missing parts can be moulded or modelled incorporating wire supporting frameworks fixed to the whole piece.

Broken parts are refixed together and to the whole, provided they are thick enough to carry drilled holes, either by pinning—which means inserting a metal pin into a hole drilled after the pieces have been stuck—or by dowelling, which is the joining of pieces by drilling matching holes in each and cementing in a single dowel. Any or all of these methods might be necessary at the same time in one single object (see Fig. 10).

Lastly, broken pieces can be riveted together. The ugliness of this technique, strong though it is, means that it has largely been superseded by other methods since the discovery of the better adhesives, and is really only used for extreme strength and utility rather than for restoration and beauty.

Cleaning. Before any porcelain or pottery may be mended it must be cleaned. Normally all that is needed is a wash in warm soapy water. If the piece is already clean, then wipe it with a piece of silk dipped in methylated spirits. Keep any old pieces of real silk for china restoration work, as silk does not leave little bits of lint or fluff caught on jagged edges.

Remove stains from china with very dilute hydrochloric acid, but test first in case the acid etches the glaze. A cloth dipped in either bicarbonate of soda or common salt will remove coffee stains.

To remove dirt along cracks which are not going to be repaired—cracks which are, and look dirty—make a pad of cotton wool and saturate it in a mild bleaching solution such as hydrogen peroxide and lay it along the crack for some days, renewing the solution as the pads dry out. When the treatment is completed, scrub the piece gently with a soft brush, and even more dirt may come away. This method is useless on earthenware, but for this and for English porcelain, which is usually so porous that the dirt is well ingrained, soak the piece for up to a week in a solution of domestic bleach. This will remove most stubborn stains and won't etch the glaze.

If china has been previously mended, the edges of the breaks may be very dirty, and sometimes glue remains which is invisible except under a magnifying glass. All edges must be cleaned, and you must be sure they fit together before going ahead with the next stages of the job. First of all soak the pieces in boiling water with pure detergent added. Remember, if there is another part of the object which has been mended and which you do not wish to do again, to keep it out of the water or it may melt apart. Glue, Seccotine, shellac and Durofix will come off in boiling water, and joins made with these adhesives will soften sufficiently to be parted. If this treatment does not tackle the old glue then you will have to get to work with the appropriate solvents (see *Solvents*). Methylated spirits will shift shellac that has resisted boiling water. Swabbing with cotton wool dipped in amyl acetate removes cellulose adhesives such as Durofix. Acetone removes cements, but may take some time about it. Dissolvex is a new solvent which will shift many kinds of glues including Araldite, especially some of those used for glass repairs.

Literally to boil a piece in detergent and water is a last resort to remove stubborn adhesive without abrasion. Finally it may be necessary to pick away at the old adhesive with a scraper or even a needle. Obviously this has to be done with care.

If old rivets have to be removed, cut them in half with a needle file and pick out the bits using acetone to remove the cement if necessary.

The first two methods are done with just a few tools, but the moment you have to drill, more complex tools will be necessary, and this means more expense, and also more time spent on learning to handle the tools. China drilling is not difficult, but it takes a light hand and a steady one, and infinite care and patience.

A power drill, which is normal workshop equipment nowadays, can be used with the right bits for a lot of drilling work provided it has both vertical and horizontal bench stands and operates at the right r.p.m. The ideal tool for most drilling is a dentist's drill—in fact an electric motor with a flexible drive and a hand-held drill at the end. But this is an expensive piece of equipment not justified unless a lot of work is to be done, so its use is not described here. A hand drill and appropriate bits will be needed for starting holes, and for the awkward holes. A special twist drill with high gearing can be bought for work on china, and some people prefer this to the other types. It is good for dowelling and for work in substantial pieces, but is a little difficult to control on really delicate work.

Brass wire is used for pins and dowels, and unless you are doing very complex work only one or two sizes will be needed. Other standard tools such as the hacksaw, and calipers you may already have. Small cramps and a pin vice are useful, and all shapes and sizes of small files and rasps, scalpels, and probes. Various materials will be needed for making moulds, supporting pieces while they dry, binding to aid adhesion etc. These I shall mention as they come into use.

Sticking. There is some general information on adhesives under that specific heading. Here I shall discuss the various methods used for mending china with adhesives.

Ordinary domestic two-tube Araldite (AV and HV 100)

is suitable for all practical purposes for almost any work. It is best used in a well-warmed room, and pieces should always be warm when joined. Keep the tubes of Araldite warm *before* mixing. All this helps the adhesive to flow readily, and to grip. A cold unheated workshop is not a suitable place. Work in a heated room with a radiator with a flat top or heat conductive shelf above it so that pieces can be kept warm.

The second important point, already stressed several times, is that pieces must be clean and dry. Pieces that have been washed or boiled to clean them may take quite a long time to dry out, especially the unglazed edges of breaks. Damp, dirty surfaces just will not adhere.

Thirdly it is vital to grasp the basic principle of adhesion, which is to bring the original faces as close together as is physically possible, with the thinnest practicable layer of adhesive between. The edges and surfaces of the break then lock together naturally. It is a misapprehension to suppose that thick layers of adhesive will make more successful joints. All the adhesive that is needed is enough to fill all the tiny gaps and crevises between the faces so that the two present smooth surfaces to each other with no air pockets, and they will adhere.

Lastly, stuck joints need to have some pressure exerted upon them while the adhesive is setting, either by clamping the pieces together, or by putting a weight on top of a flat piece, or more usually by binding the pieces together with gum strip (not Sellotape) in such a way that pressure is exerted on the join.

The methods of applying this binding differ slightly with every mend. Always use gummed strip, and buy a big roll at least 1½″ wide. Cut this down if necessary. Strips are stuck as nearly as possible at right angles across joins such as simple breaks in a plate or vase. When the join is rather more difficult, such as a broken vase handle or lid, the strip is stuck on so that it will exert pressure at right angles to the join. The wet gummed strip is easy to put into position, and as it dries it shrinks, holds fast to the china and so exerts pressure on the join. When you reach the stage of placing the prepared pieces together, wet the cut strips of paper thoroughly but remove any surplus drips of water with a swab. They should be damp right through but not dripping wet, as moisture will prevent pieces from adhering if any gets on to the broken edges. Sometimes it is best to pre-stick the strip on to one piece of the work (after you have warmed the piece for glueing, or the gummed strip will dry out completely) and then put the two edges together. Draw the loose piece of strip down smoothly and tightly across the join. A little bit of practice at binding difficult shapes will soon teach you how best these paper bandages can be applied. Remember always that as the strip dries and tightens it must pull across at right angles to the join, so bringing the pieces together and holding them there. Use very long strips if necessary. Make a cross of strips, stand a pot in the middle and bring the ends right up over the top to hold it together. Small pieces of strip may be needed across very small joins to exert pressure (see Fig. 7). A binding applied like a puttee round and round an object is almost useless except to keep things in place. The same binding techniques will be used when mending by dowelling and pinning, as described later, and a little thought and study will help you to work out the details for each job. Very occasionally it is not possible to bind, to clamp, or to weight pieces together because of a peculiar shape or a break in an odd place. Make supports out of plasticine or wire to push pieces together, or at any rate to hold them in position while the adhesive sets. No tension is applied to the joint so this way isn't that satisfactory, but it is better than nothing. Don't let plasticine come into direct contact with Araldite or any epoxy resin, as the two will react together.

Having cleaned your porcelain or china ready for mending, next check whether or not all the pieces are there, whether or not they fit together perfectly, and then decide upon your method of restoration. Pieces made of thin

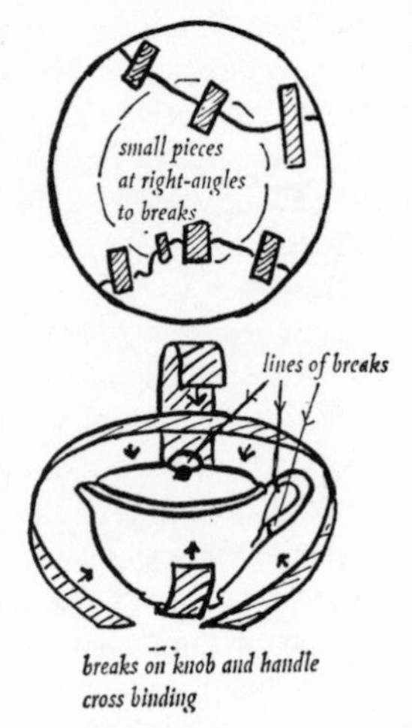

Fig. 7

china are almost impossible to dowel or pin as there is no thickness to take drilled holes. Hollow figures may need to be dowelled in the hollow sections, or by pinning. But if there are sufficient clean, close fitting edges which will contact nicely, sticking alone may be all that is needed. Details of dowelling and pinning follow, but here I deal with sticking on its own. A piece which has been broken into several pieces should be very carefully checked for fit before applying adhesive. If necessary make up a kind of jig-saw puzzle, using Sellotape and fit the whole thing together. Be careful not to work yourself into an impossible corner by putting the pieces together in such a way that the last piece cannot be got into place. This can happen, for instance, in a bowl where the break consists of two or more pieces which are wider at the lower end than they are at the rim end. If a piece is in several fragments it is sometimes easier to stick two or three pieces together to make one large piece, and then join this to the main piece. So do take a bit of thought, and be sure that you have solved the puzzle before taking any irrevocable steps (see Fig. 10).

If, as well as being in several pieces, the pot has a chunk missing, it will be necessary to mould a new piece, but first of all any sticking must be done and finished, and the moulding is later carried out as a separate operation.

Having cleaned the pieces, dried them and checked for fit, warm them thoroughly. Prepare a small amount of adhesive, no more than you need, and apply it with a knife to one edge of the two pieces to be joined. Usually it is best and easiest to apply the adhesive to the piece rather than to the whole. Put adhesive on both edges only if the fit is not perfect, or if the material of which the pot is made is very heavy thick porous earthenware, which will absorb a lot of adhesive.

Then bring the two edges together as firmly as you possibly can. Obviously you don't want to break the china again, but exert as much pressure as you dare on the join so that the adhesive comes squeezing out. If you want to remove adhesive in order to get a clear look at the join through a magnifying glass to make sure it is properly aligned, moisten a water colour brush in a little methylated spirit and take off a little adhesive with that. Do not take it right down to the join as this will weaken it. Surplus adhesive should not be removed along the join until *after* it has all set. Any adhesive which has escaped on to other as yet unmended broken edges, or on to gilt or lustre glaze on the pot, must be removed at once with the paint brush. On the broken edges it will prevent proper matching if it dries into a little lump, and it will lift gilt or lustre when it is finally removed.

H.M.G. adhesive can be used in conjunction with Araldite to make a fairly quick setting join, by putting H.M.G. on one surface of the join and Araldite on the other. The quicker drying H.M.G. binds with the Araldite and helps to hold the two pieces together while setting takes place.

Then the joins are bound with gummed strip as described above. The piece is put down and left to set. Epoxy resins, especially when the join has been properly strapped, will hold almost immediately, and the pieces will not move in relation to each other unless the joins are imperfect or unless the balance and weight of the pieces are such that gravity pulls them out of place. Plasticine supports, bowls of fine clean sand, bits of wood and wire, will all make supports and cradles. If the piece to be joined is some kind of figurine and not a plate or a bowl with flat or curved surfaces, parts sometimes have to be stuck on entirely by balance. The heads of small figures frequently get broken off, and if you intend to stick a head back without dowelling, the fit along the break will have to be perfect, and the figure itself must be held in a firm grip so that the head will balance in place while the adhesive sets. Bury the figure in a bowl of sand, with the broken edge set horizontally just above the level of the sand, and then balance the part on it. Move the buried section about until the broken-off piece balances perfectly upon it. Make sure all loose sand is brushed away from both edges, and then, using very fluid adhesive, anoint the broken edges. Carefully put the piece back into place, and allow it a few moments to adhere before delicately, and without moving the buried base, setting it perfectly into position.

It really is a matter of trial and error, and with a bit of ingenuity you can find a solution to every problem of sticking and binding and balancing.

The final process of sticking when using epoxy resin glues, is to harden the joins by baking. If an entire piece has to be moulded in, after some sticking has been done, it is still best to bake the first work for a short while before doing the moulding, just to make certain that the work which has been done is really firm. Baking can be omitted entirely if the piece can be left alone for a good long time to set.

Up to a point the heating of Araldite softens it, and if you leave a job for some hours before baking and a piece has slipped a little out of place, warm the join with boiling water swabs to soften the Araldite enough to move the piece back into position. Leave joins made with Araldite for a few hours before baking and then place the piece in the oven of an electric cooker or of a solid fuel cooker. Put an asbestos mat on the middle shelf and place the china carefully on that, and keep the oven at a temperature of 200 deg. for about an hour. Over 300 deg. the Araldite will darken and in any case the china may not stand it. If your oven has no thermometer, buy a small one. If it is impossible to keep the temperature of the oven steady, heat the oven, put in the piece, and switch the oven right off, leaving the piece there until the oven is cold.

Mending Cracks with Adhesive. So often articles crack without breaking. The cracks get dirty, and the piece when touched vibrates a little and does not ring true. It may, one feels, collapse into pieces at any moment. Cracks can be repaired quite effectively without completely breaking the pieces apart. Most forms of pottery and porcelain are to a small extent flexible, so carefully insert the edge of a razor blade and part the crack a little. Clean the crack as described above and make sure that the whole piece is thoroughly dry by standing it on a radiator until it is pretty warm. Heat the separate tubes of Araldite to get them runny and make up a mix, with a little white colouring in it if there are any chips along the crack which need to be filled. Mix the Araldite on a warm surface and keep it warm while working. My own nightstore type electric radiators which have flat tops, are absolutely ideal for this work and I work directly on top of one. This is not recommended by the makers of nightstore radiators but who cares about that!

Prise the crack apart with the razor blade as far as is possible without breaking the piece completely. If the crack runs right to the rim or edge of the piece, slide the edges of the crack apart a little, one up and one down to expose some of the broken edge. Run the adhesive right into the crack, work it in with a finger if necessary, then move away from the radiator and press the edges tightly together. Wipe off any surplus adhesive with methylated spirits, but not that exactly along the crack. Put several pieces of gummed strip across the crack at right-angles on both sides of the piece, and leave the whole thing to dry (bake after an hour if you wish to) for half a day on the top of the radiator. This should set the adhesive perfectly.

Let the repaired piece cool down completely and then soak it in water to remove the gummed strips. There will be some spots of adhesive along the join squeezed out when the join was made and deliberately not wiped away. Rub the spots very carefully with glass paper and break them down before removing them with a scalpel or a razor blade. This cleaning is quite a delicate operation and if done without abrasion may result in lifting little chips of china or glaze.

If the crack was also chipped and Araldite with colouring was used, tidy the filled chips with fine glass paper, and over-paint or glaze if necessary.

Moulding and Modelling. When whole pieces of a pot or a figure are missing, the gap can be filled by rebuilding the piece with epoxy resin composition filler. But it isn't quite so simple as that! Perfectly satisfactory pieces for plates, vases, bowls, statuettes etc. can be moulded or modelled and simply stuck into place provided the piece is not going into domestic use, but such mends are not strong enough to withstand hard wear for very long unless they are supported by metal cores or pins. It is easy to mould or model a jug handle without a core, but unlikely that it will last very long if the jug is used. If the new handle has a core it will be very strong indeed. The making of cores and pins is described in a later section, and here I shall talk about moulding and modelling without supports. The techniques involved are almost identical when supports are incorporated. The job requires only a few cheap tools until the moment when you get involved in metal work and drilling for supports. And many people, once they reach this stage, just take the work to an expert restorer rather than buy drills and bits etc.

Before mending a piece such as a bowl or plate or vase, without using a core, scratch or file the broken edges so that the new piece of moulding will lock into the edge as it sets. The danger is that your new pieces may not adhere too well to the smooth and thin edge of a break without some kind of roughness in which to get a grip, as the problems of adhesion are not quite the same as those of sticking two edges of porcelain or pottery together.

Next, a backing is necessary. This means a surface up against which you can press the filler to remake the piece. If the object is a flat plate, with a flat surface, the same gummed strip as is used for binding can just be stuck on the outside surface of the piece completely covering the broken area. As it dries it stretches tight and makes a good smooth surface up against which to press the filler. This gummed paper cannot be used on a curved surface because it pulls taut and flat across the curve as it dries. Therefore the mould will have to be made with a flexible material which will take a curve. Plasticine does the job well, but it never sets hard and can be pushed out of shape rather easily. Wedge plasticine before use—this is a potter's term meaning quite simply banging it until it has no air bubbles in it. A mallet or a wooden rolling pin make good bashers for plasticine.

If you use plasticine for the mould and Araldite for the filler you will have to get some cellulose acetate to use as a parting agent as the two react upon each other and must be separated by coating the surface of the plasticine which will come into contact with the filler.

There are other moulding materials. The dental impression compound Paribar is more expensive, but is quite excellent for the work, and is worth the extra money for it can be used again and again, needs no parting agent, and has other uses. Paribar is softened in hot water before use and resets fairly hard but is flexible enough to be extricated from quite deeply cut castings.

Making Moulds. Imagine that you have to replace a curved piece with a fluted surface, from the edge of a bowl. The whole of the edge of the bowl is fluted in the same way so you take an impression of a matching piece of the pattern on a sound section of the edge. Wet the surface of the bowl and press a slab of plasticine (about half an inch thick) on to a section just a little larger than the missing piece. Carry the plasticine up over the rim of the bowl so that it will be marked but don't bend it too far round the rim if there is any ridge or it may be difficult to remove the plasticine without bending it. Press the plasticine well and truly until you are satisfied that you have made a perfect impression. Lift it carefully off and place it over the hole on the outside of the bowl in exactly the right place so that the pattern is continuous. Press it lightly so that the broken edges of the china mark the plasticine, then remove the plasticine, and paint the area inside the edge marks with cellulose acetate parting agent, then replace it over the hole. It will stick to the dry china round the edges of the break. Bend over the top sections of plasticine away from the hole, round the rim of the bowl to keep the mould in place. A few strips of Sellotape across it and on to the china will help. Don't use gummed strip, for this will dry out and flatten the mould. The Sellotape may give slightly but will help to avoid the disaster of the mould coming off the pot in the middle of the filling operation which follows.

Paribar can be used in exactly the same way to make a mould especially where there is a deeply indented pattern in the china. The Paribar goes hard, but it can be softened with swabs of boiling water and removed from the filler section without breaking it when the job is done. No parting agent is needed so that the Paribar can be put directly on to the break and left there.

Filler Composition and Filling. Now to mix up some filler (see *Fillers and Cements*). Araldite two-tube epoxy resin is first mixed together and then titanium dioxide (or other whitener) is added until the mixture has a nice doughy consistency. This mixture is a bit sticky and clings to tools and fingers. Keep a little dish of the powder handy, and another dish of Methylated spirits. Dip your fingers in the powder, and the tools in the Meths from time to time, and you won't get so stuck up. When dried out this filler looks exactly like biscuit, or unglazed baked china and takes overpainting very well. It also sticks directly to the edges of the break and you should have no trouble in making a perfect join. It isn't the easiest of jobs to make and handle this filler, but the result is so good that it is worth practicing to get the mixture of the right colour and consistency.

Kaolin mixed with Araldite in the same way makes a very stiff, not quite so sticky, more translucent and buff coloured filler, but it has the disadvantage of not sticking quite so well to the edges of broken china as does the first mixture.

Isopon polyester resin filler is a paste which is mixed with a hardener. It is excellent for filling big holes as it dries quickly, but this means also that you must be able to work quickly. When using Isopon make an inside mould of the break as well, and having filled the mould, put the second inside mould on to the filler from the inside to get a smooth interior surface, pressing it down well. Isopon requires no parting agents. Although it will stick to itself so that it can be built up in layers, it will not stick to china, so when the moulds are removed, the new Isopon piece will come away and will have to be stuck in just like an ordinary broken piece. It can be rubbed and filed to finish it off. It cannot be used as an adhesive.

Bondapaste is another excellent filler which hardens quickly and does not have to be baked, nor does it require powder additions to make it opaque. It does not dry white, but this is immaterial if you are going to overpaint it anyway. It can be used as an adhesive or cement and when used as a filler it stays in place without further adhesives. It can be filed, carved and abraded within a quarter of an hour of use, so is a very time-saving material, once one is experienced enough to shape it quickly.

The exact consistency of any filler is difficult to describe and can only be discovered by trial and error. If it is too hard it will push the plasticine out of place as you press it into the mould. If it is too runny it will tend to run into the lower part of the mould in whichever place you are holding it, and will not make a piece of even thickness. If the mould is made of Paribar then a stiffer mix of filler can be used.

The mixture is worked into the aperture with a round ended tool. Boxwood potter's modelling tools are excellent but many things make good modelling tools. Some workers like to prop the pot up as they work, others hold the pot in one hand so that the break with its mould is cupped and held in position while the filler is worked in. Great care must be taken to make sure that the filler goes into all the corners and crevices right up to the edges, with no air bubbles trapped underneath. Smooth the inside surface with the tool and with thumbs and fingers until it is as like the surrounding inside surface as your eye can judge. Set the pot aside for an hour, if the filler is Araldite, by which time it will have set to a rubbery consistency and can be worked further if necessary. If a quicker setting filler has been used, once it has set hard it can be carved, filed and abraded until it is absolutely perfect, and it is then ready for overpainting.

To speed up the setting of a mend done with Araldite, bake the pot for half an hour at 200 deg. F. If there are any small cracks or pits in the surface fill them with a thin mixture of filler, using a water-colour brush.

Chips. The mending of chips, big and small, which do not go right through a piece, involves work which is halfway between the filling of apertures as described above, and modelling which is described in the next section.

Quite simply, you make up a mixture of any of the above mentioned fillers into a fairly stiff mixture and press it into the previously cleaned and dried area of the chip and smooth it until it looks right. Don't get air bubbles under the filling. Wheel chips—large chips on the edge of a piece—should first have a thin layer of adhesive, to help bind the filler in place. The art of filling chips is to get a good blend along the edges and to get the filling neither too proud nor too shallow, and in getting the composition in so that no air bubbles remain behind to raise it in due course. If you suspect that a little air is trapped, prick the filler with a pin and press it down again and fill up the pin hole.

Allow the filler to dry out over a hot radiator and then, when it is hard, rub it down with glass paper until you are satisfied that the chip, after overpainting, will be indistinguishable. Pick up the piece and squint at it at eye level in all possible planes, and rely on the sensitive tips of your fingers run across the mend to detect any irregularities. If even at this late stage the chip is not properly filled, more composition can be added for it will stick to itself, and the process repeated until you are satisfied.

Modelling. When neither straightforward sticking, nor press moulding can be used to mend an object, try modelling. It is impossible to make a mould for a missing piece which is not a repetition of another part of the object, as described previously. The missing piece just has to be built up from scratch and the result depends on the artistic ability of the restorer. Large modelled sections will have to have metal supports—dowels, or pins, or strips—and the techniques will be described later on. I am still concerned with the techniques which do not include drilling.

When a part of a plate, or a vase, or perhaps a lid knob must be remodelled, take a piece of rather doughy filler composition and roll it either flat for a flat section, or into a ball for a knob, or into a sausage for a handle, in an approximate size and shape for the job. Then press it firmly to the edge of the broken part, and model it with Boxwood tools, fingers and any suitable home made tools that you may fancy. Whenever epoxy resin mixtures are being used, dip the tools in methylated spirit to avoid sticking.

Modelling becomes really interesting when a porcelain object such as a figure or perhaps a vase festooned with flowers and leaves has pieces chipped out or broken off and lost. To remake flowers and leaves is not at all difficult. Any woman who has ever made an apple pie with a decorated crust knows the technique. The pastry, in this case filler composition in a nice doughy mixture, is rolled out to the thickness of the petal or leaf required and then pieces are cut out of it in the flat. A small sharp knife or scalpel can be used as a cutter, shapes having been first marked out with a darning needle or a fine graver. Or, if the leaf or petal pattern is to be repetitive, a cutter can be made out of strip brass or copper foil, bent to make the appropriate shapes. Make a template or pattern out of plywood, using a fretsaw (see Fig. 8). Tack this pattern to your work bench with a central nail and then hammer a copper foil strip round it with a small hammer until it is exactly the same shape. If the template is pinned with a central nail it can be pivoted round as the cutter is being made so that all pieces can be reached.

The cutting of different species of flowers, daisies, roses, apple blossom etc. is hard to describe exactly. It is a matter

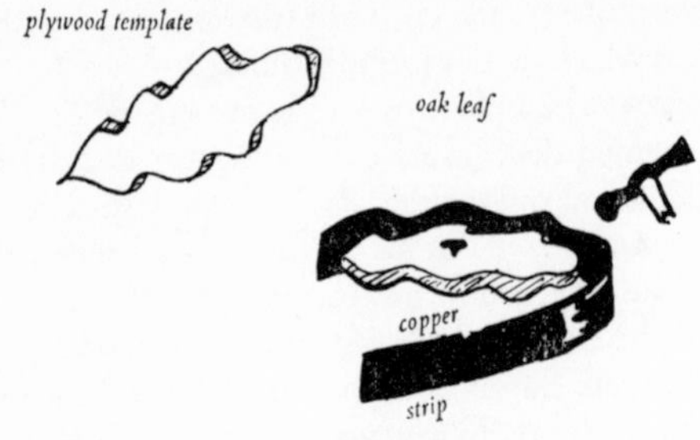

Fig. 8

of careful observation of the petals which are to be matched, and of measurements with calipers and dividers, if your eye is not good enough. Petals are cut out in flat shapes and bent over slightly at the edges, and rolled into concave shapes etc. Once your petals and leaves are made they are then fixed to each other and to the main piece, and there is no great difficulty about this unless the anchorage point is very small indeed, especially if you are using a good adhesive filler composition such as Araldite and titanium dioxide. It is often possible to add an extra leaf, or to put in a small support of composition disguised in some way as part of the decoration, which will hold the modelled part in place. Most people have a collection of tools for modelling which they have made specially to get into different corners; sewing needles, bent knitting needles, scalpels, spatulas, rifflers, spikes and blades of all kinds, even old hacksaw blades, come in useful.

When pieces of an object are missing for which no pressed mould can be made, it is still possible to make a mould out of plasticine which approximates pretty closely the missing piece, and to put this on to the whole in such a way that the aperture can be filled with composition in exactly the same way as a pressed mould is filled. Then the new piece must be rubbed and shaped to final perfection after the setting or baking process has been completed; but this can be a slow job.

There are problems when it comes to modelling difficult things like faces; it rather depends upon how clever you are, but there is yet one more way, which involves modelling. It is a much more complex and tricky job, but it can save such a lot of time and trouble in the long run, and once again may enable you to get away with it without resorting to pinning and dowelling.

Make a model, in plasticine, of the missing part. Actually this is easy if you have a talent for modelling, terribly difficult if you haven't. Say for instance that half a leg and a foot are missing from a figurine. Using calipers and dividers, measure the other leg and foot exactly, so that at any rate he won't have a size six left boot and a size ten right boot. Then model a plasticine leg to the right dimensions and in the kind of position in which it looks as if it ought to be, and keep trying your model in the space until it satisfies you. Plasticine doesn't harden so take as long as you like over making the model.

Having made your plasticine model, a mould must be made from it and a cast or pressing taken from the mould. The finished cast can simply be stuck into position (or dowelled or pinned if necessary).

Take a sheet of glass, and a large lump of plasticine. Roll the plasticine out into a very thick strip and lay it on edge on the glass (see Fig. 9) in a square or a circle plenty big enough to hold the model, horizontally. Then fix the model, horizontally, halfway up one side of the container that you have just made. A peg carefully inserted into the end of the model and pushed out through the container side should hold it into position. Then prepare some plaster of Paris. Into another container which can be handled easily and has a pouring lip, put enough water to half fill the mould container, and sift plaster of Paris powder into it until the mixture is the consistency of thick cream, stirring with the hand to break up lumps. Then pour the plaster of Paris mixture into the mould until it is halfway up the model. Leave the whole thing to set. Then cut two wide grooves or shallow holes out of the plaster. Next, thoroughly soak the surface of the plaster with soft soap liquid, making

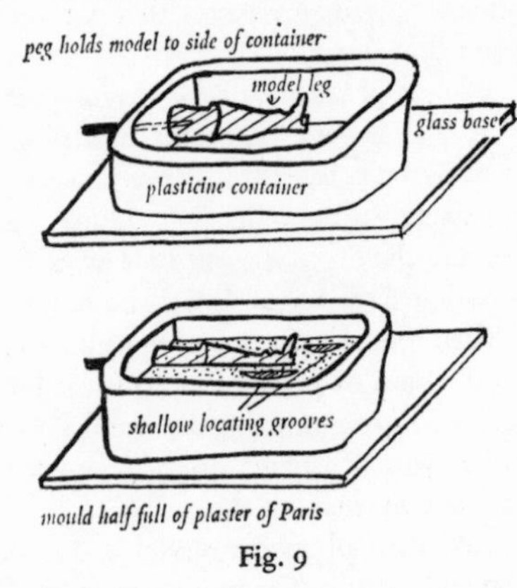

Fig. 9

sure that it is really well drenched and that no tiny part has escaped swabbing. This acts as a parting agent between the two halves of the plaster mould. Make another mix of plaster as before and pour this into the mould until the model is well covered. When this has set, remove the plasticine case and ease the two sections of the casting apart. Take out the original plasticine model and you should have a perfect mould in two halves. This mould will have two locking pieces where you cut the grooves or shallow holes so that when the two halves are put together again they will locate exactly, and at the end where the model was attached to the side wall of the plasticine container, there will be a hole.

Now you have a mould which can be used to make a casting or pressing of your original model. Smear a film of silicone grease all over the pattern sections of the mould to prevent the filler sticking to the plaster of Paris, and then make up enough filler composition to fill the two halves of the mould. This filler should be soft enough to flow freely into the mould sections. When the two sections are filled, bring them together and bind them tightly with wire. Ram the composition well home, through the hole. Leave the mould, with the hole at the top, for two hours to set, and then, if you are using epoxy resin, bake it for half an hour at 200 deg F.

Undo the wire binding and take off the plaster. If you have not used a parting agent, the plaster can be cut out and broken away and the last of it scrubbed off the model. Stick or dowel the finished model to the whole, having made sure that the edges fit perfectly by filing and abrading. Any discrepancy in fit which is too big to be put right by filing, can be filled with some filler composition.

Moulds can also be made from pieces of porcelain similar to the piece you are trying to replace, and then pressings made from these can be carved, filed, abraded, and built up to fit exactly.

Instead of plaster of Paris, rubberised solution such as Qualitex can be poured around your model. The advantage of using this material is that the mould is flexible and will come off difficult undercut models without damaging them. Rubberised solutions, therefore, are best for making moulds from models which must not be damaged in any way. The technique is much the same as that described above. A plasticine container is built up round half the part to be copied, and the solution is poured in.

The process is repeated on the other half and you then have the complete mould in two sections. Details vary with each job.

Faces on statuettes are very alike, and differ only in detail of hair and headdress. There is no reason why, if you collect figures, you should not make a series of moulds or masks from any statuettes that come your way, and so build up a stock of faces in reserve for the day when they may be needed.

Incidentally, the principles of making casts, moulds, pressings etc. are generally similar for work in all kinds of materials, and many restorers of objects other than china, such as old guns and pistols, make their own metal castings. It is a skill which has so many applications, not only for restoration but for creation. Modern materials make exciting castings and pressings, and it is an art well worth studying for its own sake.

Metalwork in China Restoration

Now for the techniques involving metalwork and drilling. There are three main types of drill, the hand drill or Bob drill; the hand twist drill, or the power drill.

Bob Drill. The Bob drill, which is the traditional china restorers' tool, consists of a steel spindle with a bob of wood towards the lower end, an eye at the top, and a tapered point at the bottom. It has a cross bar of wood with a hole in the middle which lets it slide up and down the spindle. A lace is passed through the eye at the top of the spindle and fastened to each end of the cross bar.

The cross bar is held by placing three fingers on top of it and the thumb and little finger below. Make a small starter hole in the china with a broken file or a diamond and place the point of the drill, which carries a tube containing a drilling diamond, in this hole. Keeping the drill upright, press down gently on the cross bar. This moves down the spindle, unwinding the lace and turning the spindle complete with bit. The impetus of the bob, acting as a kind of flywheel, carries the rotation of the spindle a little further as the pressure is relaxed and then back again rewinding the lace onto the spindle. Keep the drill straight, don't let it sway from side to side, and lubricate the bit with oil as the work goes on.

Hand Twist Drill. This is used much the same way, although it is for some people not quite such an easy tool to use. It is necessary to exert a little pressure to get the bit to bite, and the piece must therefore be firmly held.

Power Drill. Provided your drill runs at about 2000 r.p.m. it can be used for drilling, especially in substantial pieces. The hole will have to be started by hand. Special bits are needed, and the drill must be mounted vertically on a bench stand. For some jobs a horizontal stand will have to be used. If the piece is properly held under the drill, and you are not too heavy handed, this method should be satisfactory.

Tack some kind of pad to the workbench under the drill to act as a shock absorber. This should not be too soft; a piece of thick lino or cork will do.

Put the drilling tube into the chuck of the drill and start the motor, checking carefully to make sure that the tube when spinning is absolutely straight and not whipping at all.

Put the piece of china on the bench under the drill and bring the machine down, not switched on, to within an inch of the working point. The hole should already have been started with a hand drill. Get everything perfectly aligned and secure the piece to the bench as best you can. Start the drill and bring it very very gently down into the hole. The moment it bites, lift it and have a look to see if you are working straight. Then lubricate with water (or turps if you are drilling glass) and continue drilling, lubricating frequently. To drill large holes, start by drilling a small one, then enlarge the mouth of the hole for the next size drilling tube with a tungsten carbide bit. This means a lot of bit changing, so don't forget to check for whip each time.

To keep objects steady under the drill, prop them up with large chunks of plasticine. Small objects can temporarily be set in plaster of Paris, in a small wooden box at the right angle for drilling. If your piece of china is so big that there isn't room to get it under the drill, it may be possible to swing the drill round so that it points out over the side of the bench, and then the china can be put on a separate table at the right height.

All drilling takes a steady hand, a straight eye and a light touch. If the drill waves about the results won't be very good, and if too much pressure is applied there is always a risk of splitting the china. This applies especially when using a mounted power drill, as you have so much leverage and it is harder to tell by feel just how much pressure you are putting on. Practice on some useless bits and pieces, for hours, if necessary!

Dowelling. Dowelling is the joining together of two pieces by boring a hole in each, the ends of which match exactly, so that either a straight pin, or a pin angled at the join (as in a knee joint) can be cemented in to hold the two together. For most purposes half hard brass wire 132, in a $\frac{3}{32}''$ diameter hole, is right. The holes should be about a quarter of an inch deep. To align the holes properly, bore one side, then push the tip of a thoroughly wet indelible pencil into the hole so that it is well ringed with ink. Then bring the other, undrilled side to the join tight against the drilled piece in exactly the right position. The indelible ink will mark the undrilled piece, and you can go ahead and bore right on the mark. Countersink one or both holes with a slightly bigger bit.

Take a piece of brass wire and flatten it slightly on one side to allow air to escape from the holes as it is inserted. Push it home into one of the holes and cut the wire, allowing sufficient length to go to the bottom of the other hole. Then fit the second piece over the wire. If the wire is too long to allow the faces to come together properly, snip off a little tiny bit and try again until you do get an exact fit. Obviously, the secret of this job is to be sure your holes are accurately bored facing each other, or you will spend ages fiddling about bending the wire or enlarging holes.

When the wire fits properly, take the wire right out and lay it on the work bench and roll a rough file backwards and forwards across it so that it is scratched and scored to make a key for the cement.

Make up some cement (*see Fillers and Cements*) from whichever mixture you fancy. Araldite and titanium dioxide or kaolin or whiting are as good as any because Araldite sticks so strongly. Fill one of the holes, that on the bigger piece of china and push in the dowel making sure that it goes right home as it did when you fitted it. Some cement will ooze up into the countersinking. Wipe it away, as the countersinking will later fill with cement from the other side of the join and this will help to hold the two pieces together. Try the second piece over the dowel just to make sure that everything still fits. Then remove it, and leave the dowel to set hard in its cement. The next day, or after baking for half an hour at 200 deg F. if epoxy resin has been used, clean the surfaces of the break with methylated spirit, and make up some more cement and fill the hole in the second piece. Provided the broken edges of the piece fit perfectly it is not necessary to put adhesive between them. Adhesive will in effect widen the join a fraction and make a line which will show. But if there are irregularities or missing chips, then put some adhesive or even a little filler composition in to fill them out. If you decide that adhesive is necessary, put a thin layer on one side of the break only.

Push the second piece well home on to the dowel, and make sure that the fit is good. Bind the pieces together with gummed strip as described before.

Dowelling is used to join modelled or moulded or cast pieces to the whole in exactly the same way. Dowels will also support joins in hollow china, or help to join hollow pieces to solid pieces. The solid piece is bored in the same way as before, but the reverse process has to be carried out in the hollow section, a block of cement being built up to hold the dowel. When both sides are hollow and the hole is large use a heavier gauge wire or make a dowel out of a tube of brass. It is difficult to fill in a large space with cement and to set a small pin in the middle of it. Wrap a ribbon of cement composition round and round the dowel until it is enough to fill the cavity, and push the dowel, with its cement wrapping, firmly into place. The cement may ride up the dowel if it is too much to go into the cavity, and it will not adhere if it is too little. Having cemented in one end of the dowel, leave it to set, and then swathe the protruding end in the same way, finally fitting the broken piece over the dowel and cement, until a flush join is achieved.

Pinning. In some ways, pinning is easier than dowelling. A hole is drilled through the broken sections *after* they have been stuck together and a pin, prepared in the same way as a dowel, is pushed into the hole which has been filled with a fairly liquid cement mixture. The advantages of this method are that there is no difficulty in getting the holes to match up as they are drilled in one go, and that no binding is necessary as the join has already been made. The pin is sunk well into the hole so that the outer end is just below the surface. The hole is then filled in with composition and overpainted in due course (see Fig. 10).

Cores. Cores are commonly used when a large missing section has to be built up, to support a piece which may sag

Fig. 10

or be liable to breakage. Wire of a suitable gauge is used according to the thickness of the china. Holes are bored each side of the aperture, only just deep enough to accept the end of the wire. A piece of wire just slightly longer than the gap is cut and roughened, and sprung into the holes. Or a piece of wire is put into each hole and joined in the middle by soldering. Several pieces of wire can be put across a gap if necessary. If the part to be replaced is curved, a teapot handle for instance, a correctly shaped core of wire is set into holes at each end of the break (see Fig. 10). Shaped cores can be made as skeleton frameworks for almost any shape or size of missing piece. Sometimes a core is not fixed at each end, but is a dowel set in the edge of a gap (see Fig. 10). A bent pin makes a skeleton limb on which to build up a whole piece by modelling.

All these techniques can be combined with those described under the headings of *Sticking*, *Moulding* and *Modelling*.

If the china is thick enough to carry drill holes, and it is intended to make a press mould out of plasticine or Paribar, a core or cores can be put across the gap to strengthen the new piece, the filler composition being carefully tooled in to cover the wires.

Cores can be a great help when modelling. It is not possible to make a model direct by putting a large lump of composition over and round the core, it will just slip about the wire. First wind a ribbon of composition round and round the wire, and leave it to set hard. Then do the modelling on this compo base.

Overpainting. The art of overpainting mends in china so that the repair becomes indistinguishable from the original is skilled indeed! If you cannot paint anyway, then it is going to be pretty difficult for you. The work is done with good quality water colour paint brushes, and you will need several sizes, particularly some good fine ones. Artist's oil paints are fine because they can be mixed so easily to make absolutely any colour. Reeves Artist's Gel makes a good medium, or clear enamel glaze if you can get it. If you want the work to dry out quickly add drying agents bought from Artist's Colourmen. Just how glazed

Fig. 11

the final result may be depends upon the medium, but the final result can always be varnished if it is not glossy enough. For work where opaque colours are needed, polymer paints are ideal and can be mixed with their own glaze medium to get a high finish. Darwi Italian Glaze is also excellent for work on china.

Many school teachers know about the modelling compound made by Darwi, and this firm now make a most excellent range of paints for their modelling compound which can be used on china to give the effect of glazes without firing. Darwi transparent paints are available in twelve colours, and there is a similar range in opaque paints. Both types of paint when dry should be given a coat of the special Darwi Varnish, as this gives it the ceramic lustre, and dries hard to give lasting protection. They also make metallic paints called Darwi-Or and Darwi-Al in gold and aluminium.

The normal technique for building up colour to re-create glaze is to start by painting the whole area with a ground colour which exactly matches the ground colour of the original. This may be anything from black to white, but will probably be fairly opaque and will contain a lot of white. After this layer has dried, further layers of more transparent colour are built up over it until the decoration matches the original. To explain in detail how this is done would be to embark on a course in oil painting. As a simple example, flesh colour is made up of at least five colours. White, a little grey or blue, black, yellow, and crimson. If you mix all these colours together in any proportions the result will be an opaque putty coloured paint. Applied in transparent layers very thinly, first white, and then the lightest touches of blue, grey and black, and then a little yellow and a final coat of transparent palest crimson, it will build up beautiful flesh tones. The portrait painter learns all about this, and if you are going to do much of this kind of work a good book on oil painting techniques could be helpful.

Perhaps I have made overpainting sound too difficult—but it isn't really, and it is great fun, and astonishingly good results follow just a little practice.

Here is a list of colours which will cover any range you want and will come in useful for other restoration jobs. You might even get interested in painting in oils, if you aren't already. Anyone who has an oil paint box will have enough colours and will know enough about painting to go ahead without further purchases except medium. Dry powder pigments in several of the tints below are also very useful for all kinds of restoration work. It isn't necessary to have all these colours. For small jobs just buy the ones you need and so build up a stock piecemeal. Polyurethane glaze gives a good hard clear finish if a high gloss is required.

Colours. These should be Artist's oil and *not* Student's oil colours.

Titanium White
Ivory Black
Cobalt
Naples Yellow
Yellow Ochre
Burnt Sienna
Burnt Umber
Rose Madder
Indian Red
Deep Cobalt Green
Chrome Green
Paynes Grey
French Ultramarine
Cerulean
Winsor Lemon
Raw Sienna
Raw Umber
Venetian Red
Cadmium Red
Viridian
Permanent Green

GLASSWARE

Wash glass with liquid detergent in warm water, and brush cut glass gently with a soft brush. Dry it and polish it with a silver cloth. If badly stained cut glass is left to soak overnight in warm water and detergent with a few drops of ammonia added, the dirt will probably come off. The cloudy deposit left on glass by lime in water is the devil to shift. Fill the glass with distilled or rain water, *not* tap water, and leave it for a day or two and then scrub gently. If the lime still persists a little spirits of salt may shift it. Spirits of salt is a pretty good shifter of all kinds of stains, and it also makes neat little shot holes in your clothes if you spray it when brushing!

Bad stains will usually yield to a soaking in a five per cent solution of caustic soda. Metal polish will remove stains on glass. Decanters and bottles with stains which will not yield to brushing or which cannot be reached can be cleaned with sand, preferably silver sand. Put in a small handful of sand, some detergent and a little warm water, enough to allow the sand to swirl around when the bottle is shaken. A careful swirl or two should abrade off the stain. A five per cent solution of nitric acid will clean off wine stains.

Scratches on glass will sometimes respond to a good polish with jeweller's rouge. Glass is a strange substance which does in fact flow, and rubbing with rouge does actually make it flow and fill in the scratches.

Removing Stoppers. Glass stoppers sometimes get firmly stuck in old decanters and glass bottles, and brute force is the worst possible way to shift them. Make up a mixture as follows:

2 parts alcohol
1 part glycerine
1 part common salt

Paint this on the stopper, particularly where it enters the bottle or decanter, and leave it for a day. A few gentle taps should then shift it. If this doesn't work, heat the decanter over a stove, or stand it on a radiator so that the air inside will expand, and force out the stopper. This method will have to be used if a stopper has broken off short in the neck of a bottle. Keep the piece that comes out for it may be possible to repair it.

Making Lamps out of Bottles. Large glass jars and carboys can be made into lamp stands and this job always looks best—

if the jar is to be filled with solid or semi-solid matter such as pebbles, or sand—if the flex passes up through the bottle. If the jar is to be filled with liquid, obviously there are difficulties in preventing leakage through the flex-hole, and in keeping the flex totally insulated from the liquid. Outside fittings are best and safest for liquid filled jars.

Bore holes in glass jars exactly as they are bored in china. The safest way is to start by boring a $\frac{3}{32}''$ hole with a diamond drill, lubricating constantly with turpentine. Then enlarge the hole with successively bigger drills until it measures $\frac{3}{16}''$, which is big enough to take the flex. Start each bigger hole for the follow-up drills with a tungsten carbide bit, and don't push through too fast or the glass will split. Just let the drill grind gently away. A little practice on a spare milk bottle is advisable if you haven't done the job before.

Mending Glass

Sticking. On the whole glass is stuck together in the same way as is china. There are one or two small points of difference. The edges of broken glass are very smooth and some roughing up with a diamond scratcher will give the adhesive a better key. Gum strip is used to put tension across the joins as described in the section on sticking china. This is very important when mending glass as a very tight fit is essential to ensure adhesion. When the adhesive has set, surplus which has squeezed out is removed by rubbing it down with steel wool, *not* glass paper as this would scratch the glass. Remaining adhesive can be lifted off with a scalpel or a razor blade.

Wine glasses so often break across the stem, and such breaks can be mended with Araldite, but won't be particularly strong because glass tends to break again near the point of the first break even if the join itself holds firm. Stainless steel bands are sometimes put round stem-breaks, but this is an expert job and the band must be very accurately made so that it can be sprung over the stem and glued tight round the join.

Dowelling. Dowel glass as you dowel china. This is a better method of mending a wine glass stem. The dowel will show, but inside the stem the Araldite/titanium dioxide cement looks rather like frosting and is not unsightly. Glass is more fragile and shatters more easily than china, so take just that much more care when drilling.

Glass that has been mended with epoxy resin can be heated to speed up setting, but remember that glass breaks if exposed to sudden changes of temperature. Therefore it must be put into a cold oven and the heat brought up gradually to about 150 deg. F. Then switch off the heat and without opening the oven door leave it to cool right off again. The draught caused by opening the door would crack the glass. After an hour the oven should be cool enough and the adhesive set. Only white clear glass may be heated; coloured glass cannot be stoved and the adhesive will have to be left to harden in its own sweet time.

Moulded Repairs. Glass can be repaired with liquid acrylic resin, of which there are several makes on the market. Technovit 4004A dries to a clear glass-like material. It can be polished and it can be coloured. Acrulite and Tensol Acrylic are two other very good materials for this work.

Make plasticine moulds as described in the china section, but always use white plasticine as acrylic will take up colour from coloured plasticine. No parting agent is needed unless the makers of the acrylic so state. Technovit is made up by adding hardening liquid to a powder, and it is then poured direct into the mould, care being taken that there are no air bubbles present or the effect will not be clear. Warm the glass a little before pouring the filler as acrylic gives off heat as it hardens and might crack cold glass.

Acrylics can be bought ready coloured, or can be tinted with powder pigments and made opaque so that it looks like china, rather than glass, so it is quite useful for repairing china of a self colour which requires no further overpainting. Jasperware may be repaired satisfactorily with acrylic.

Surplus acrylic is cleaned from the edges of the join immediately, while it is still liquid. It can be abraded and rubbed away after hardening but this dulls it and there is the danger of scratching the surrounding glass. Acrylic can be polished with silicone carbide spaced grit cloth or paper, grades 150, 240 and 320.

Sometimes you may need a large lump of pseudo glass for a restoration. Acrylic can be poured into a mould, but this means that a model must first be made, and then a mould as described in the section on casting and pressing china parts. It is much easier, really, to make the lumps out of Perspex as this material is worked in exactly the same way as wood, and turned on a lathe. The tools—saws, files, drills etc. are lubricated while working with ordinary soap, and the Perspex will have to be polished when all shaping has been done.

Pieces of chandeliers can be replaced with Perspex, and new pedestals made for glass ornaments (see under *Perspex*).

CLOCKS

I once knew a cottage kitchen which boasted seven clocks. They all worked, and they all kept fairly good time, but

Fig. 12

they were not synchronised and four of them chimed. Twelve noon was a time of fantastic, explosive excitement. One by one the clocks went into action. The plaster flaked off the ceiling, the several cats scattered in all directions. The clocks went on chiming for about three minutes, and one was left in no doubt at all as to what time it was. The owner of the clocks picked them up for pennies at farm sales, and dismantled them by the light of an oil lamp, cleaned them and put them together again. Usually that was all they needed, plus a little persuasion and persistence, to get them going. I don't think John ever actually made a new part or mended an old one; he may occasionally have used a part from another useless clock, but that was as far as it went.

The moral of all this is that as far as the movements are concerned the amateur may well succeed in making an old clock go just by careful cleaning and oiling; but if there is a broken part it must be replaced or repaired and this *is* specialist work. There are plenty of books in any local library about clock cleaning and repairing, and a few evenings' study of the descriptions therein of the various types of movement, escapement etc. will help you at least to have a vague idea of what you are doing when you start dismantling clocks.

Not long ago I inherited an old Norfolk clock. It had hung on the wall in my mother's home all my life, and for the last twenty-five years to my certain knowledge had not worked. I felt that it had in some way 'died' and that it was only fair to try to resurrect it. When I inherited it, although I had never tampered with a movement before, I felt that as the thing wasn't working anyway I couldn't do much harm. The case of the clock is about four feet long, and it hangs on the wall. It has a very heavy lead weight, which once, when I was a child, fell through the bottom of the clock with a cataclysmic crash when the gut broke. This accident coincided with the double pneumonia of a much loved uncle, and was taken by my family as a sign that he had died (and presumably twanged the gut in passing). He recovered and lived for years, which destroyed my faith in such omens for the rest of my life.

All this is a little beside the point. First I removed that weight by lifting the pulley off the gut. I removed the hood of the clock by sliding it forward, complete with glass door, and laid it aside very carefully. It is a pity to break a perfectly good glass, although should you do so, or should the glass be broken, a glass merchant will cut a new one, and it can be reputtied into place, or cemented in with Araldite. The round glass in my clock is puttied into the wooden front in exactly the same way as a window, except that the putty is on the inside. Then I took out the pendulum. Having removed the hood I could see the back of the escapement and the top of the pendulum with its suspension spring (see Fig. 12), and it was simple to take out the pendulum without breaking anything. Lastly I removed the whole movement and face complete on its seatboard. Sometimes the seatboard is screwed to the body of the clock and these screws must obviously be removed first.

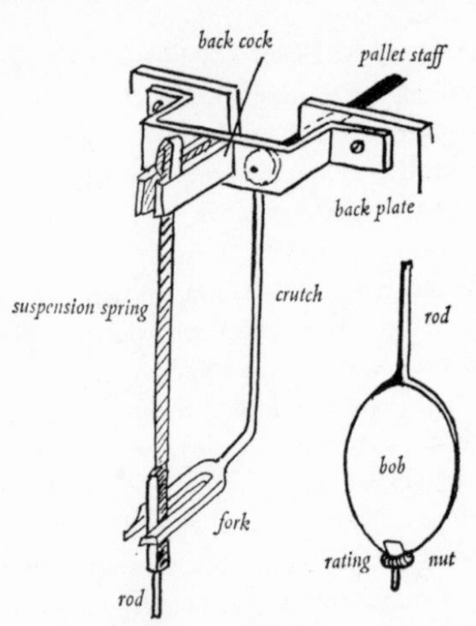

Fig. 13

Don't take the works apart just for the fun of it—only just as much or as little as is necessary to get at them to clean them. Start with the hands, which on a long case clock are held in place by a small pin above a metal washer. Before the face can be taken off, the hands are removed. Then take out any pins or latches holding the dial plate pillars in the front plate of the movement. Clean all the parts well. Steel parts may need a little rust remover on steel wool, or fine emery cloth. If brass parts have been lacquered and look horrible, strip off the lacquer with methylated spirit, as it is probably shellac. Clean the brass parts carefully with metal polish. Rub steel parts with black shoe polish. Replace old gut lines either with new gut or with nylon or stranded steel, so that the weight will never fall down again as mine did and frighten you half to death, smashing the bottom of the clock into the bargain.

Hands may be reblued with special fluid, or by laying them in sand and heating until they become blue all over. Mend broken hands with silver solder; soft solder is not strong enough for such tiny joints and will melt if the hands are reblued. Rusty blued hands held in the flame of a candle become black all over. Move them in the flame all the time until they are well coated, and then paint on a thin coat of clear lacquer with a soft paintbrush so as not to disturb the colour. An Aerosol lacquer spray will do the job even better. If the hands are still warm the lacquer will flow on and blend nicely.

I discovered in my clock that some idiot had screwed an ordinary coat hook onto the frame to anchor the gut, which then ran down to the weight and up to the drum. This had the effect of making the weight hang slightly to one side of the case, and I am sure was one reason why the clock did not go. Keep your eyes open for this kind of tampering. I removed the hook and anchored the gut through its original hole. Tie the gut above the hole with a knot with a loop, and slip a little peg through the loop so that the knot cannot slide down through the hole.

Broken or hopelessly worn parts must be remade or rebuilt, and this is expert work. Study a good book on clock repairing if you wish to start on this metalwork.

Having made sure that there is no more dirt, old oil, damp or rust anywhere in the clock, reassemble it. Touch each bearing first with a drop of clock oil, using a long feather or a piece of copper wire flattened at one end as a dropper. Don't use machine oil, and be sparing with the oil. Mineral oil left on brass surfaces causes staining. Never put any oil on the teeth of any of the wheels.

Replace the hands and make sure they move freely, but not so freely that they drop by their own weight. If they are too loose on their arbour, tap the outside brass washer lightly all round, so bending it in just a little, until the hands hold on the arbour.

If the brass face of a clock with engraved lines filled with black wax has been overpolished, and the black removed, replace it by making a mixture of shellac, methylated spirit and lampblack, painted back into the engraved parts. Let it set and then wipe off the surplus with a mild abrasive. Jeweller's rouge or whiting on a soft rag taken right across the surface should do the trick. Then polish well. The resilvering or regilding of clock faces is a highly technical business, but brass faces can be polished and painted with clear lacquer such as Ercaline. If the clock is not too valuable, you might try regilding or resilvering the face with one of the modern restoration pastes or paints as described in the section on gilding.

Reassemble and set up your clock properly or it won't go. The movement on its seatboard is replaced in the clock and the hood put back. Check that the face of the clock is centrally positioned behind the glass door, then take off the hood again so that you can see what you are doing, and put the pendulum back. Put it through the door in the trunk, and up through the gap in the seatboard and through the crutch. Very carefully feed the suspension spring through the slit in the back cock, and pull it gently downwards on to its seating. The pendulum swings freely with the block on the pendulum below the suspension spring, free in the crutch. Rehang the weight and wind up the clock (see Fig. 13).

Now make sure that the clock is upright. A weight on a piece of string will give you a plumb line by which to judge. Check the fore and aft level with a spirit level. Make sure the clock stays firmly in its place, using wedges if necessary.

Then swing the pendulum and start the clock. If all is well the tick-tock will be equal and solid. If the clock is not set right the tick will be louder than the tock or vice versa, and the time interval will be noticeably unequal. Provided the clock is set level, the best way to get the pendulum swinging right is to bend the crutch slightly. Face the clock, place the first finger of the hand on the loudest tick side at the top of the crutch. Place the first finger of the other hand at the bottom of the crutch on the other side, and then bend the crutch gently with the lower finger, towards the louder tick. When the tick is equal, the clock will keep going.

If the clock gains, unscrew the rating nut at the bottom of the pendulum, thereby lengthening the pendulum as the bob drops. If it looses, shorten the pendulum by screwing up the nut. A pendulum length of 39½″ should give a tick of exactly one second!

Longcase clocks usually have nice mahogany or oak cases. These may need repair and cleaning, and the section on furniture should be consulted. It is a pity, unless it is unavoidable, to strip down the case of an old clock. The patina which it has acquired over the years is irreplaceable.

Any simple clock can be dismantled, and cleaned by brushing the parts with petrol or benzene, rubbing them dry and reassembling them in the reverse order. The trick is to be able to dismantle in the right order and then put it all together again. I have no room to go into the details of dismantling even half a dozen of the simplest movements, and suggest that you borrow the Cassell's *Work Handbook* on clock cleaning and restoration (or buy it). Just one point that I must make—do be careful if you try to dismantle a clock with a spring. If the mainspring is wound up—and it well may be for people usually wind up a clock that won't go and then it is left that way—don't loosen *anything* until the spring is unwound, or it may fly out and damage the clock or you quite severely. The spring is unwound by putting the key on the winding square and holding it firmly. Lift the ratchet pawl or 'click' and let the key turn back half a turn. Drop the click so that it re-engages and holds the spring. Take a fresh grip on the key and repeat the process until the mainspring is unwound. Then you can go ahead in safety.

Dust does clocks no good, and some clocks have a kind of fretwork panel to allow air to flow freely. These frets were originally backed with fine mesh fabric to keep dust out, and that gets filthy or torn. Replace it with clean fine meshed material. Synthetic material won't do unless it has an open mesh for it does not allow the passage of air. Very fine nylon curtain material does quite well. By the same token cracks or openings in the clock case should be sealed wherever practicable with filler or by rebuilding. Even strips of brown paper or Sellotape X inside the clock will do.

Clock Keys. Missing clock keys are not too hard to remake. How beautiful you make your new key is up to you, but in its simplest form a clock key usually has an open square end which fits over a square spindle. I have used copper tubing to make a key for a long case clock. Sheet brass or even a piece of tin can be made into a tube and soldered

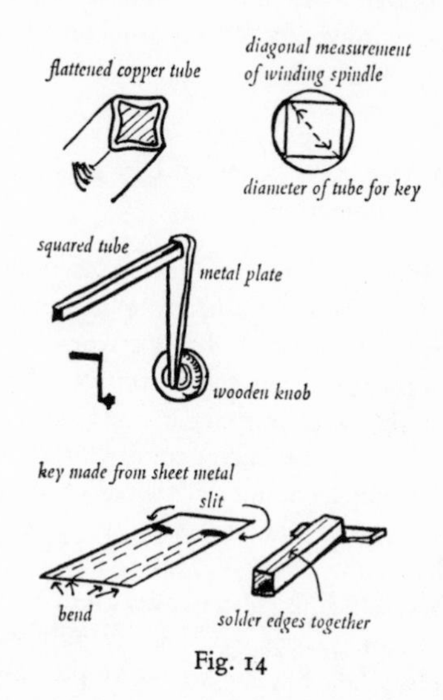

Fig. 14

before flattening it to fit. The measurement of the spindle from corner to corner diagonally across the section, is approximately equal to the interior diameter of the tube needed (see Fig. 14). The end of the tube will flatten out to make a bow, or it can be mounted on a piece of wood, or attached to any kind of handle you may fancy.

When cutting a piece of sheet metal to make a key, leave a flap to form a handle (see Fig. 14).

COINS AND MEDALS

Coins should not be cleaned unless it is absolutely necessary. They loose a lot of value through faulty cleaning, and it is just as important to know when to clean as to know how. Get a book out of your library on coin collecting and study it before cleaning any coins, if you know little of the subject.

Gold Coins. Wash very dirty coins in soap and water using a stiff bristled brush very carefully. Dry gold coins with a soft cloth or soft leather.

Silver Coins. If silver coins are not in exceptionally good condition and are rather worn, removing the ingrained dirt will often make them look a lot worse! If they are tarnished to a blue or green colour, this gets damaged by too much washing and brushing up, and most collectors prefer to leave well alone. Silver coins which are in really good condition but have uneven toning or are just plain filthy, should be treated either with carbon tetrachloride or trichlorethylene (see *Solvents*). This is dabbed (not rubbed) on very gently, and immediately afterwards the coins are washed in running water. On really ugly toning use Goddard's Silver Dip but do not wash the coins afterwards or they will look too highly polished. Don't rub coins with the polishing cloths provided with cleaners. Ammonia in ten per cent solution will also remove stains, the coins being washed immediately after application; otherwise a whitish skin will appear which will ruin all your careful work.

Copper coins. Verdigris on copper coins is often caused by cigarette ash dropping on to them, and although this is hard to remove it can sometimes be done by soaking the bad part in olive oil and scratching the verdigris off with a bone needle. Don't use steel needles for they scratch the surface of the coin. Don't use solvents on copper coins, just clean them with a stiff bristle brush used quite dry.

Copper, silver and bronze coins and medals can also be cleaned by immersion for a very short time in a solution of five per cent nitric acid. Do this with great care for the acid will etch metal, particularly copper. Take the pieces out after one or two seconds and wash them immediately under a running tap. If only a part of the coin is corroded, protect the rest of it from the acid with a coat of wax or grease before immersion in the acid, and then wash it thoroughly. Polish coins with a little lanolin grease or Renaissance wax polish.

DETERGENTS

Detergents are the modern substitute for soap, and are perfectly suitable for many cleaning jobs as they so readily remove greasy dirt. However, some of the commercial brands sold as washing powders, or as liquid washers, have added ingredients of some kind: scent, colour or 'whiteners'. While china, glass and pottery can be cleaned quite safely with these, they are often not suitable for cleaning other materials, and where detergent is recommended it is best to use a pure detergent such as the following:

Teepol
Boots Liquor Sulphestrol
Lissapol N.

Detergent can be mixed with other chemicals to make an emulsion which will spread and penetrate easier that way—

for instance carbon tetrachloride and benzene mixed with one per cent Lissapol N for cleaning some kinds of stonework.

ENAMEL

Enamel is a type of glass with added colours in the form of metallic oxides. This is fused to the surface of metal objects.

Enamel on metal may be of three different types: painted on to an enamel background; Cloisonné, which is done by soldering fine wire to the metal surface to shape the designs, and then infilling with enamel; or Champlêve where the same effect is achieved by cutting shallow cells into the surface of the metal to take the enamel. In all types, an object is then fired to fuse the glass and enamel.

Enamels should be kept away from direct heat, as the glass will expand at a different rate from its metal base and stresses will be set up which may result in the enamel lifting or crazing. Enamel on metal which doesn't like damp, such as copper, must be kept dry otherwise corrosion may form on the metal and lift the enamel.

To restore enamels, use ordinary artist's oil colours, and where chunks are broken off, a good imitation can be made by adding colour to Araldite, or to a thick solution of celluloid in amyl acetate, or to Durofix.

Having retouched the colour, enamelled objects can then be lacquered with Frigilene, or painted with thin acrylic, which will reseat any lifting pieces. Once the lacquer has soaked right in and dried, so that it has filled any cracks and cemented down loose pieces, wipe the surface of the enamel very carefully with a piece of cotton wool wrung out in acetone. Be careful that no liquid acetone runs into joins etc., or it will undo the repair work that has just been done. If enamel has at some time been repaired with animal glue, it may have gone slightly mouldy. Wipe the joins with Santobrite before continuing with retouching and lacquering.

Don't try to refire enamel, it just won't work.

FABRICS

All textiles come under this heading, and generally the cleaning treatments depend upon whether dyes have been used or whether the fabric has simply been bleached or whitened. Cotton and linen have usually been bleached, and go very yellow with age. If the fabric is in good condition use very dilute domestic bleach to rewhiten it, then thoroughly rinse the article in several changes of clean water. Reckitt's Blue may be added to the last rinse. Delicate articles made of muslin or lace, which are in a fragile state, cannot be given such rough treatment. A powdering of French chalk or Fuller's Earth, later brushed off, will remove some stains and grease marks. If the article is attached to a cushion for instance, this may be the only way of dealing with it. Lace which can be detached should be placed in distilled water for a while to loosen the dirt, then put into fresh water containing a little pure liquid detergent and soaked again. Paddle it gently up and down in the water if the dirt is stubborn. After careful rinsing, spread the lace on to white blotting paper and pin it flat, and put it in a warm place to dry. It is important to pin lace properly in shape or it may distort during drying.

Muslin garments such as old doll's clothes or old baby clothes are best washed very carefully in a mild solution of detergent, and should not be rubbed, but gently paddled up and down. It is most important to rinse the garment two or three times in clean distilled or rain water. The garment should be rolled in absorbent paper and ironed flat when it is nearly dry.

Coloured fabrics which are not colour fast can be cleaned with carbon tetrachloride. Heavy embossed material will be considerably brightened by brushing with a mixture of four parts benzol and one part methylated spirit.

Test for colour fastness by laying the fabric over white blotting paper, and then patting it carefully with a swab of damp cotton wool. If the colour runs it will show on the blotting paper underneath. If the material is old, the dyes are probably vegetable in origin, and likely to run, so should only be washed in cold water.

To remove large stains on this fabric, place the piece on clean blotting paper and then drop a solvent into the centre of the stain, which will spread out and go through on to the blotting paper carrying the stain with it.

To remove stains on textiles, provided the stain can be identified, try the following treatments, always with care and a minimum of rubbing.

Alcoholic Drinks: Wash in warm suds. Sponge with surgical or methylated spirit.

Beer: Soak in a hot solution of 2 teaspoonfuls of sodium sesquicarbonate (water softener) to 2 pints of water, and rinse out well.

Blood: Fresh stains. Soak immediately in a solution of 1 teaspoonful of salt and 1 teaspoonful ammonia to 1 pint of warm water. Then wash out in warm suds, and rinse.
Old stains. Try soaking in ammonia solution, 1 tablespoonful to 1 pint of water.
Or try a solution of ½ teaspoonful of ammonia with 1 part of 20 volume hydrogen peroxide with 4 parts of cold water.

Soak for just half an hour if the fabric is coloured, as long as necessary for white or colour fast materials.
On cottons and linens, but not on silks or wool, oxalic acid solution, 2 level teaspoonfuls of crystals in 2 pints of cold water, mixed in a china or glass container, can be dabbed on and removed by rinsing within ten minutes.
Silk or wool should be soaked in a solution of salt and water.

Coffee: If washing does not remove it, try hydrogen peroxide as for blood.

Cosmetics: Clean with carbon tetrachloride. Lipstick can sometimes be lifted from washable fabrics by smearing with vaseline and then washing in warm suds.

Egg Stains: If they won't wash out, soak in a solution of salt and water, or try one of the proprietary digestive types of stain removers, such as Big S., Biotex or Radiant.

Fruit and Berry Stains: If they won't wash out they can be removed by working a few drops of glycerine into the stain, leaving it overnight and then damping with a few drops of white vinegar, and then washing out with warm water after two minutes. Cherry, pear, peach, plum and other stubborn fruit stains in cotton or linen can be bleached out with hydrogen peroxide solution as for blood. Soak the stained spot for a few minutes and then wash it out in sesquicarbonate, ½ teaspoonful to ½ pint of water.

Glue: Must be removed with solvent. Acetone or nail varnish remover will probably shift it.

Grease: Such as butter or candlewax. Wash in water with a little ammonia added. Put fabric under blotting papre and iron. Sponge with carbon tetrachloride.

Indelible Pencil: Sponge with methylated spirit.

Ink: Ballpoint ink can be removed with methylated spirit. Indian ink must be sponged with methylated spirit and then rubbed with glycerine. Repeat the treatment until the stain lifts and then wash with detergent and water. Old Indian ink stains are there for ever! Writing ink, the same treatment.

Mildew: This is difficult to remove. Washing thoroughly in sodium sesquicarbonate may help.

Nail Varnish: Remove with amyl acetate or nail varnish remover.

Paint: Emulsion paint; soften it from underneath with amyl acetate, then rub off, and work in a paste of soap and water and wash well. Oil paint, dried; carbon tetrachloride or benzene on the underside till the paint has softened, then wash out as above.

Rust and Ironmould: Try oxalic acid treatment as for blood. Rust remover can be used in extreme cases, but must be tried with care and washed out thoroughly.

Shellac: Soften with methylated spirit.

Shoe Polish: Bleach out with hydrogen peroxide.

Fig. 15

Soft Drinks and Syrups: Sponge with surgical spirit and water, or dab with glycerine and leave for 1 hour before washing out.

Soot: Make a paste of carbon tetrachloride and flour. Smear on the stain and let it dry, then brush it off.

Tea: Soak and wash with sodium sesquicarbonate. Then bleach with hydrogen peroxide if still visible.

Varnish: Soften with amyl acetate.

Wine: Bleach with hydrogen peroxide with a few drops of ammonia added.

See the section under *Insects* for trouble from clothes moths.

FANS

All kinds of materials were used to make the hand fans so popular with our grandmothers, and many of them are very pretty things, well worth repairing.

Fans were made of ostrich feathers set in ivory or ebony; or of bone, ivory, or ebony, or of paper and silk, mother of pearl, or lace. Some fans have a ribbon tie running through

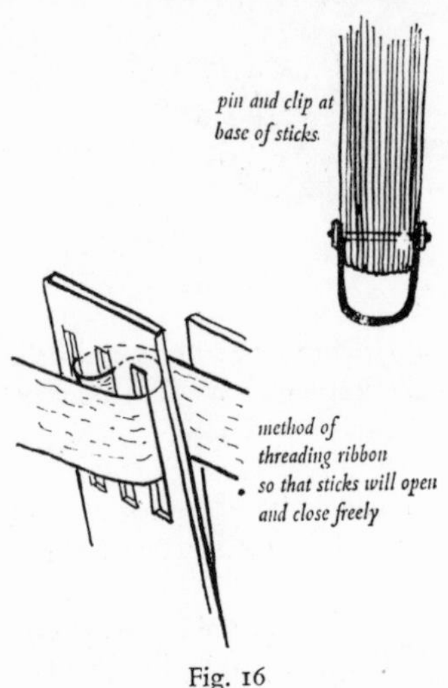

Fig. 16

the sticks which controls the spread, and this ribbon may be torn or very dirty. It is simple to replace the ribbon, but it will probably be threaded in such a way that the fan may be opened and shut easily without pulling or looping. Take a careful note, when removing the old ribbon, of the way the threading is done so that you can put it together properly (see Fig. 16).

To clean fans made of ivory, bone, tortoiseshell, ebony etc. treat as described under *Ivory* and *Tortoiseshell*.

Broken sticks present a problem if they are made of these materials, and very careful sticking with epoxy resin is the best way if you have all the pieces. A strengthening piece may be added, either of matching material if available or of clear plastic. Replace broken wooden sticks by making a careful copy. Remove the D-shaped ring at the bottom which holds the sticks together if a whole new stick is to be inserted. The straight part of the D is a pin through the sticks, and this will have to be taken out (see Fig. 16). If it is riveted through, file back the sides of the rivet at one end until the pin slips out. Put the new stick in its correct place. The pin should be hammered a little to lengthen it so that it can be riveted over when replaced.

Clean fans made of fabric by brushing with Fuller's Earth. Immersion in any kind of liquid is usually inadvisable because there will be glue about which can all too easily be loosened. Painted colours on fans may not be fast and will run, or be lifted, so take care. Remove spots carefully with dry cleaning fluids such as carbon tetrachloride, or blot out grease spots as described in the section on *Needlework*, remembering once again that heat will melt any glue.

Mend torn paper fans as described in the section on *Books*, or put in whole new pieces of paper as detailed in the section on *Prints* and *Watercolours*, and revarnish with Winsor & Newton's Water Colour Varnish if necessary. Sometimes a heavier varnish will have to be used, and Picture Mastic Varnish or Copal will match this.

Generally speaking, fans are delicate objects which need a lot of care and delicate work, as each one must be treated on its merits according to the material from which it is made.

FILLERS AND CEMENTS

Fillers and cements are used for the repair of china, glass, wood and occasionally metal. Adhesives are also used as fillers and cements, with the addition of a little colouring matter or powder to give them colour, body or both.

Plastic Padding. Described in the section on adhesives, this makes a useful filler for metalwork because of its colour, and it needs no further additives for this work. It is not usually used for china restoration work.

Wood fillers. There are several makes of plastic wood which are used as fillers for small holes in woodwork.

Wood filling compounds of various kinds and in various colours can be bought, in proprietary brands, and these are tenacious and excellent. When dry, fillers can be sanded to a smooth finish. Epoxy resin fillers such as Araldite, suitably coloured with dry powder pigments or oil paints, can be used as fillers for rebuilding small missing sections of woodwork. The slow drying of some types makes them rather difficult to use, and care must be taken that, in larger repairs, shrinkage does not leave hair cracks between the new pieces and the old.

Various compounds are used for filling, and making casts and pressed moulds, and for modelling new pieces where it is not possible to make moulds.

Bondapaste. This is an excellent adhesive filler which can be built up on itself in layers, and when hard can be worked with files and gravers. It is a good filler and cement for china restoration needing no additive. It dries quickly so any moulding or modelling must be done fast.

Isopon. This is a paste filler which is mixed with a hardener. It dries quickly and doesn't shrink under heat, and it needs no parting agent to separate it from the mould. It can be fined and abraded with glass paper and other abrasives. It sticks to itself so it can be used in layers, but it does not stick to china, so after hardening and removal of the mould, it must be stuck to the china with Araldite, exactly as if it were an ordinary broken piece. It can only be worked for about ten minutes before it becomes too tacky, but this is an advantage when you are fairly practised and it can be used for quite large pieces without internal support as it sets fast, so will not sag so readily as a slower setting filler. The fact that it will not adhere to plasticine also allows props and pads of plasticine to be used to support it while it is drying.

Plaster of Paris. Widely used for the making of moulds, it is quick drying and easy to handle, but it is not suitable by itself as a filler, being too soft and porous.

Seccotine with dental plaster. A hard setting adhesive mixture which is very useful for small repairs to gesso where the object is never going to come into contact with water.

Cascamite with dental plaster. Another good mixture, which can be cut and shaped with woodworking tools, provided it has not dried out completely (see *Adhesives* for details of Cascamite). It has the disadvantage that it must be stuck into place as it is not self-adhesive. It is most useful for filling Alabaster which it matches perfectly.

Araldite. The two tube epoxy resin adhesive described in the section on *Adhesives* is the most versatile filler, having but two disadvantages. It is rather sticky to use, and it dries very slowly so cannot be used for large unsupported pieces. However, it sticks so well to the object being mended and, when set, it approaches so closely the appearance of biscuit china, that many restorers prefer it to the quicker setting compounds. It can be mixed with whitening, or kaolin or titanium dioxide to make a filler for china. Mixed with these same materials, it is also an excellent cement for use when dowelling.

Sawdust, stone powder, metallic powder, colouring pigments, either dry powder or oil paint, will all mix with Araldite to simulate almost anything you like to name. It will blend and adhere to the whole piece and strengthen it enormously. In the old days, plaster of Paris was used for this kind of building and restoration, but it was not strong or waterproof, whereas epoxy resins are both. An example mentioned in the section on *Arms and Armour* is the building up of an old worm-eaten gunstock with epoxy resins coloured to match. It can be injected by hypodermic syringe into wooden holes or cracks where it will strengthen and preserve. Unfortunately it will not take a very high polish which may limit its use.

Fillers for Glasswork. Modern acrylic resins, which are usually powders with which a liquid is mixed, are ideal for glass restoration and repair, as if mixed with care so that there are no air bubbles present, they set to a transparent, very slightly yellow material which is as near to glass as you can get. Acrylic resins can be coloured with dry powder pigments to simulate coloured glass or china, and some can be bought already coloured.

Tensol Cement No. 7 and *Acrulite Cold Curing Resin* are two excellent products in this range.

Technovit 4004. This is another versatile acrylic resin mentioned several times in this book. It can be used, mixed fairly thinly, to coat things made from cane or wickerwork to strengthen or preserve them, and to mend glass or certain types of china. With care it can be mixed with dry powder pigments to simulate Jasper ('Wedgwood') ware. Acrylics are not particularly difficult to handle, and in fact they are great fun to experiment with. They make excellent solid 'glass cases' for small objects which you wish to preserve. The technique for doing this is not within the scope of this book, but it is easy enough to work out for yourself, bearing in mind normal casting techniques!

Use acrylics according to makers' instructions in so far as mixing etc. is concerned.

Gilder's Compo. Invented by the Adam brothers, it has ever since been used for all kinds of moulding work instead of woodcarving, and is still a most excellent material for repairing moulded picture frames or some types of moulding on furniture and fittings.

Recipe 1.
- 1 lb. Scotch glue
- 2 lbs. resin
- 1 gill real turpentine
- 1 pint linseed oil
- whiting

Dissolve the glue in a gallon of water. Boil the resin, the turpentine and the oil together, and then add to the glue and water. Boil the whole lot together until the liquid has reduced a little, so that the mixture is not too runny. Add this to the whiting powder in a bucket, stirring constantly until the whole has the consistency of dough.

This recipe makes a lot of compo, and quantities can be uniformly reduced to make smaller amounts.

Recipe 2. 3½ lbs. glue
1½ pints water
1½ pints white resin
1½ pints raw linseed oil

Boil all the ingredients together for half an hour, and then add to a bucket containing whiting, rather as one adds milk and eggs to a bowl of flour when making batter. Mix until the compo has the consistency of dough.

FLY MARKS

Fly marks can be scratched off many objects with a sharp knife or even with the point of a needle. Chalk mixed with a little ammonia will remove fly blows from a hard surface such as stone. Fly blows on glass or any surface which will not be damaged by it can be removed by washing with a five per cent solution of caustic soda, followed by rinsing. Solvents such as petrol or benzine will remove fly marks, but will also remove varnish, so be careful.

Fly marks on prints can sometimes be removed by alternate baths of hot and cold water in that order, and then drying out between pieces of blotting paper.

FRAMES

Painting and Texturing. Picture frames come in all shapes and sizes, complicated and simple, and there are just as many techniques for restoring and renovating them. They can be cleaned and painted with varnish or matching paint, gilded, given two-tone or antique finishes, textured or spattered. It depends a great deal on the type of frame which of these methods is used, and also on the picture, which could well be killed by an over-weight frame or one coloured incorrectly. The frame should never be lighter in colour than the lightest part of the painting. Don't put a white frame round a picture which does not contain white. If the frame is too glossy, the highlights distract the eye from the picture itself. Frames can also be made into trays, by adding a suitable centre, or into mirrors. Frames for watercolours, pastels, or photographs, which have glasses, should be as simple as possible so as not to overpower the picture.

First clean the frame thoroughly. On a simple wooden one, detergent, water and sandpaper all carefully used should remove old grease and grime. While the frame is drying, the type of repainting or decoration can be decided upon. If it is a plain frame in good condition, a light rub down with a fine grade of sandpaper will probably be all that is needed before a new coat of varnish is applied. Of course the varnish can be taken off, and the frame left in its natural wood state and just lightly rubbed with wax polish, but if the old surface is stained or badly scratched, the new coat must be opaque, and some kind of paint is the answer. Ordinary household paint or plastic emulsion in a suitable colour looks quite well, but with a little more trouble, really exciting finishes can be obtained, and in most cases a broken finish definitely looks best.

Polymer colour water based paints made either by Rowney under the trade name of Cryla, or by Reeves under the name of Polymer colours, are particularly useful, as they can be applied very thinly producing a pickled effect over stained wood, or else thick as squeezed from the tube, and then figured, or used for two-tone work. Polymer paints contain water and should be water thinned to the required consistency, not with turps or white spirit. They dry very rapidly, but if you want to slow down the process, use the special retarder. The colours, which come in the full range of artist's oil paint colours, mix very well, and when dry will have a slight sheen, which is excellent for frames. A gloss medium is obtainable, or, although it is not really necessary as the paint is quite waterproof when dry, it can be overpainted with a polymer varnish to keep the frame in first class condition for years. Any tools or brushes used to apply the polymer paints should be washed thoroughly in water before they dry out, but if this is forgotten, a soaking overnight in methylated spirit will do the trick. Acetone will also dissolve these colours.

Texturing with polymer colours is not too difficult. The paint should have the consistency of thick cream. It should be painted on to the frame fairly thickly and, while it is still sticky, textured with a comb, toothbrush, an old wire brush, or anything else you can think of that would scrape interesting patterns in the paint. A little practice on an odd scrap of wood painted with polymer, will give you some idea of texturing. Another method is to put on different coloured layers of polymer, letting each one dry before adding the next, and cut through these with varying pressures to get the colours showing through at different levels. Diagonal, cross, mitre or lengthwise strokes can be used, and if you get really ambitious, all sorts of curved lines and squiggles. Another way of texturing is to paint the frame with polymer, and then while it is still sticky, sprinkle on a little sand, or rice, or any other small hard grained substance, shake off the surplus, and when dry overpaint with another thinner layer of polymer, and then finish with polymer varnish. A small sponge gently pressed into sticky paint will also give an interesting finish, especially if the two-tone effect is desired, using a double layer of paint. Spattering gives a nice spotty effect and should be applied over the plain basic colour on the frame by gently tapping a water paint brush loaded with the colour you want to apply. To make large spots hold the brush near the surface, and with a little experimentation the size of the spots can easily be adjusted.

One very useful process for finishing off plain frames or parts of ornamental ones is to rub on colour. This gives a nice soft finish and it is particularly good for insets, which can look far too hard and glaring against a light toned picture. Any oil based paint can be used and a handkerchief should be lightly smeared with this, and then the surplus paint rubbed off on an old piece of newspaper. The lightly charged cloth is rubbed gently on the frame, and the pressure increased until the right effect is obtained. The cloth should be recharged as necessary, but never too much as the more sparingly paint is applied the softer the finish will look, and it is not necessary to work it in too evenly. Burnt sienna is a particularly good colour for insets. If you want a simple gilded effect a paste made by Reeves called Restoration or an American product called Treasure Wax Gilt do an excellent job. They come in many tones of gold, bronze or silver, and are very easily applied with a cloth or finger on to the cleaned surface. If a bright finish is required, it should be put on fairly thickly and allowed to dry completely before being rubbed down with a soft cloth. This method is by far the best way to touch up any old gilding as the application of gold leaf is really an expert's job (see *Gilding*).

Antiqueing. Antiqueing by drilling holes, by hacking chunks with a knife, and even by taking swipes with a heavy piece of chain, are common enough practices with disreputable dealers, but any old frame bought in a junk shop will probably have enough natural blemishes to make this unnecessary, and it all sounds rather too violent. Applications of different paints can make almost any frame look a lot older and more interesting than it really is. Coats of paint are rubbed on in irregular patches and then smoothed down lightly with fine sandpaper. Deep depressions can be left dark, and bright colours should be put on sparingly. Yellow ochre, chrome yellow, raw umber, venetian red and burnt sienna, are all suitable colours, and when they have dried out and been sanded down, a thin coat of burnt sienna diluted with turpentine is overpainted, and later spots of gold or silver Restoration or Treasure Gilt can be rubbed on in small areas, or the whole frame spattered. The effect of old gold leaf can be obtained by painting the frame with a thick layer of venetian red, and then repainting with a good quality bronze paint such as Treasure Gold Liquid Leaf. When it is dry, it should be rubbed with steel wool until the red shows through in places. Restoration wax can be used instead of the bronze paint, just put on rather unevenly, but it must be remembered that genuine gold leaf gets rubbed off in natural wear and tear on the raised surfaces, while the depressions will keep the gold, and it is not so easy to get a natural finish without any rubbing off.

Mending. Old picture frames get pretty knocked about in junk shops, especially when the pictures have been removed and the glass broken. Usually it is the corners which go, the whole frame wringing in all directions. Corners can be strengthened quite easily (see Fig. 17). If the glue and the tacks which secure the frame have gone, take the frame to pieces, and remove the remains of the tacks and clean off

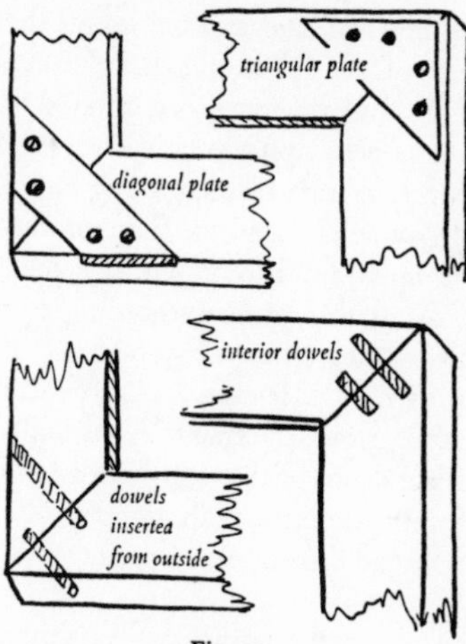

Fig. 17

the glue. Sand the faces of the corners down to the natural wood, so that you have a clean surface to work on, and then put an impact adhesive, on both faces of the corners and leave it for the time specified by its makers before bringing the two faces together. In order to get good right-angled corners, use a corner cramp. These can be bought at hardware stores and are so useful that I really do suggest that you get one and do not try to square the corner any other way, although it can be done. One method is to work with the frame on its face. Put the two faces together and square the corner using a try square to measure it and then tack a thin piece of wood diagonally across, so that the frame is held rigid until the join has set. This will hold the corners accurately, but will not put any tension on the join. To hold the corner, in addition to the adhesive, drive tacks in diagonally across the join, making sure that you don't use tacks so long that they come right through the other side, and also try to get them into the thickest section of the frame. Small holes can be drilled across the corner, and a wooden peg inserted. If you mean to do this, it is best to drill the hole with the frame held tight in the corner cramp, before putting on the glue.

If it is not possible to mend the frame in this way, or if you do not want to dismantle it entirely, the corners can be dowelled, or a plate can be screwed on to the corners, at the back. Depending on how big and heavy the frame is, put in a strip or triangular corner plate (see Fig. 17). If a strip is used, sink it into the frame by cutting right across the corner to the depth of the strip with a tenon saw, and then chipping out the piece with a chisel. Wooden strips and plates are better than metal ones, and plywood is fine for the job.

If you wish to make a frame smaller, this can be done without separating all the corners. Measure opposite sides to the correct lengths, at opposite ends, then cut through the two corners using a mitre box, and rejoin (see Fig. 18). When measuring frames, always remember that the edge of the frame overlaps the glass and the picture, and that you must allow for this when measuring. It is easier to measure your picture and/or glass, and then measure the frame at the inside edge of the rebate which takes the picture.

Mending Moulding. If the plaster moulding of a picture frame is really badly damaged, you can always strip it all off and just use the basic wooden frame. A power drill with a rough sanding disc will take off a lot of the old plaster quickly, but some of the awkward angles will have to be done with a hand scraper.

Clean all mouldings with a hog's hair paint brush, a sponge and methylated spirit. Never make a frame too wet or the plaster may dissolve.

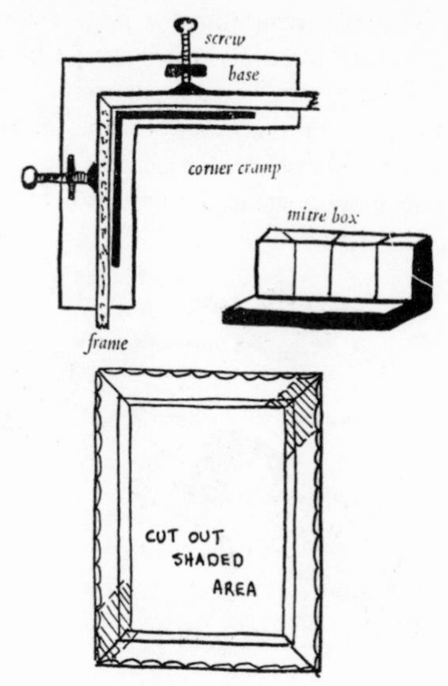

Fig. 18

Plaster mouldings are all too often broken off in great lumps. Replace these quite simply by making a moulding from an identical, but unbroken section of the frame. This is done in the same way as pressed moulding for china (see Fig. 19). Make a mould with plasticine for small sections, and then cast a piece by pouring plaster of Paris in the mould, or preferably for small sections by making a filler with Araldite mixed with kaolin powder (use a parting agent in this case), or Cascamite and dental plaster, and pressing this into the mould. The pressing is allowed to harden and then, before it is so hard that it will not stick, is carefully put in place on the break. A little straight Araldite adhesive on the face of the broken part will help adhesion. To make a mould of a large section, or one which has any undercutting which would hook round a plasticine pressing, use dental impression compound (Paribar) and make a pressed mould with this, first greasing the moulding with vaseline. Paribar can be reused many times, and no parting agents are needed before putting in the plaster of Paris filler.

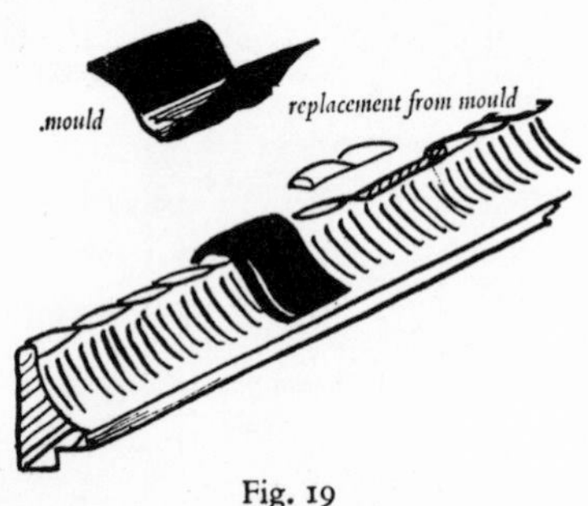

Fig. 19

Gilder's Compo can be used (see *Fillers*) and this is recommended for extensive work. It has many other uses for moulding of all kinds and is the traditional material—superseded, but not necessarily improved upon, by plastics and resins.

Gesso, in varying thickness, is used as a primer for frames, and if you are remaking mouldings with Gilder's Compo, paint it with two coats of Gesso before putting on any kind of paint or gilding. Gesso can be bought in tins (see *Gesso*).

The mouldings can also be made in Isopon or Bondapaste filler, which dries much more quickly than Araldite. It is a matter of personal preference, really. All these materials make mouldings which when set can be cleaned up with needle files and abraded with glass paper until they are satisfactorily smooth.

Framing Pictures. If you are fortunate enough to find a frame which will exactly fit a picture then all that has to be done, once the picture and frame are clean and tidy, is to put the one into the other, and to make it secure. Never put screws through the stretcher and canvas of a picture to hold it to a frame, nor should nails be bent so as to apply tension directly to a canvas.

When framing a print or a water colour or anything which is mounted on card, as opposed to a canvas on a stretcher, place another piece of clean card behind the picture to support it and to flatten it, and then put a series of small pins into the edge of the frame, to hold the lot in place. To keep the picture dust-free and to keep out insects, moisture etc., stick a piece of clean brown paper right across the back of the frame, making sure the seal is complete. A strip of wide Sellotape X or gummed strip right round the edge will make a neat job. Hardboard makes a good backing board, but don't use plywood as it is the woodworm's favourite food.

Old paintings on boards are framed in much the same way, but canvases on stretchers or tacked on to a wooden frame need a little more work. If a canvas on a stretcher is slack, tap the wedges lightly to tauten the canvas, but don't overdo it. Put the picture into the frame, and secure it with carefully sited brads through the edge of the stretcher sideways into the frame.

If your frame is too big, it can be made smaller as described above (see Fig. 17), or a mat mount of some kind can be made to reduce the central area. A mat, which is often used on a print or water colour, is simply a piece of card with its centre removed which is put over the picture as a kind of cardboard inner frame.

Having carefully marked out the piece you wish to cut out of the card, which is itself the size of the frame, get a ruler with a bevel edge and a Stanley knife (see *Tools*), and cut the board with a bevel. Special mat trimmers can be bought from artists' suppliers. The secret is to cut the bevel the same all the way round and to get the corners neat. The knife must be perfectly sharp. It is difficult to stop the ruler from slipping about, and a strip of very fine sandpaper stuck on the bottom of it will help. The bevel edge can be gilded if liked.

The mat is placed on the picture, which in turn has been put on a mount which is bigger than the hole in the mat. Photographic mountant is excellent for this job, either the paste type, or, if there is no danger involved in heating your picture, the type which is painted on with a brush and then bonded by pressure with a warm iron.

Mounts are just pieces of card on which the picture is stuck; the mount being big enough to fit the frame exactly.

Linings are rather more complex, and can be most effective, both for bringing a frame down in size, and for making a picture look better. A lining may be just a strip of gilded wood inside the main frame, or it may be a wider inner frame covered with material such as linen or velvet or sheet metal. The wood inner frame is made exactly to fit the rebates of the main frame, and is mitred at the corners. The covering material may be stuck or pinned to the lining. In order to make a neat job at the corners, it is usually best to cover the pieces before joining them.

One last word—always check wire, cord and screws used for hanging up pictures—more often than not the wire is rusted, the string is rotten, and screw rings are rusted or loose. It can be a little disappointing if two weeks later all your hard work on painting, moulding and mending together with that expensive piece of glass end up in a shattered heap on the floor.

FURNITURE

Polish

Before wood can be polished, it must be clean, and most junk furniture is pretty greasy and filthy. Your first impulse may be to strip it all off and start again, but that might be a pity if there is a decent patina under the dirt, and if there is not too much structural damage to mend. Stale beer or vinegar are good old fashioned cleaners for polished furniture, so is pure detergent in warm water. When using these water based cleaners be careful not to let water seep into joins or under marquetry or veneer, as it will swell the wood and the glue and cause no end of trouble.

Find out what kind of polish has been used before deciding what to do next. Test a part of the furniture where a spot won't show. First of all rub the spot well with turps to remove any wax polish. Next test the surface with methylated spirit, and if it is French polish, it will soften, while other varnishes and modern varnishes will not be affected. French polish can be shaved thinly with a sharp blade, oil varnishes produce thicker shavings, and cellulose varnishes won't make shavings, only powder.

Renovating French polish. Originally furniture was treated with oil and beeswax and just rubbed until it acquired a fine finish. Later, French polish, which is made of shellac dissolved in spirit, became fashionable for its hard shiny surface which seals the wood. To my mind it is no substitute for the patina which results from constant waxing and polishing, but French polish is so common that it is necessary to know how to cope with it. Modern synthetic varnishes will give much the same kind of hard shiny finish as French polish.

French polish can be improved by washing with warm water and soapflakes, and then when it is thoroughly dry by applying a reviver:

Alcohol	5 parts
Linseed Oil	2 parts
Real Turpentine	1 part

Work this mixture over the surface with a soft pad, using a circular motion.

If French polish has crazed or broken into small cracks, it may not be possible to save it and you will have to strip it right off with strong ammonia, or with acetone, or with a proprietary varnish remover, but first you could try to save it by reintegrating it, or by padding it. In any case, if the polish has a lot of deep scratches or marks you may be able to get rid of them in this way. Having tried the above reviver, which should soften the surface, allow it to flow a little and reamalgamate, next try treating it with neat methylated spirit, or methylated mixed with a little cellulose thinner. Paint the liquid evenly right across the surface of the piece.

Padding is a process whereby a fresh finish is put on over old finishes and scratches and small holes are filled up as you go. Padding lacquer is rubbed over the surface of the piece with a fad, or hard cotton pad made out of wadding (see Fig. 20). The padding lacquer is put in a saucer and the fad is charged and the lacquer is applied in much the same way as French polish (see below), with continuous circular or figure-of-eight movements, finishing with up-and-down movements. You begin by exerting light pressure and end by rubbing hard, as it is the friction of the rubbing which sets the lacquer. There is a disadvantage to this method

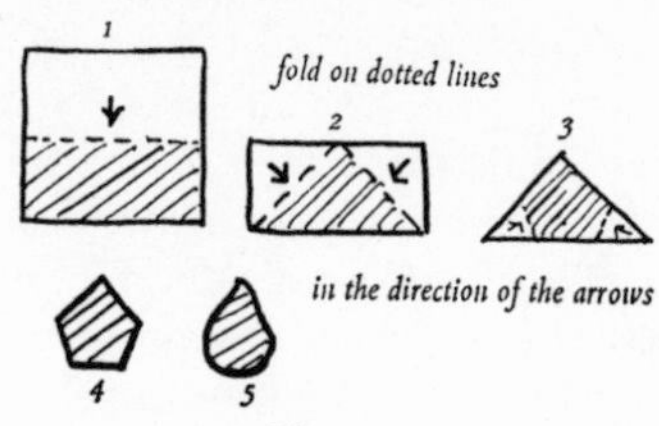

Fig. 20

and this is that it takes practice to apply the lacquer without the fad sticking to the surface and leaving marks. In the first place, the fad must be applied to the surface with a kind of light gliding motion, and the rubbing movement must be kept up continuously until the fad is removed, also with a gliding-off movement. If you do stop, even momentarily, there will be a mark and you will have to paint the whole surface over with the lacquer, or clean it all off and make a fresh start.

When you have put on enough lacquer to cover the blemishes and achieve a uniform surface, go on rubbing until the whole thing shines. It should be nearly dry by this time, but can be left for a short while to harden off. If a mirror finish is required, that is that, but if a softer sheen is needed, rub down with fine steel wool, and then polish with ordinary polish.

These two methods, reamalgamating a surface or padding it, will work well on various kinds of varnished surface, especially shellac.

However, if a varnished surface is really bad, it will probably have to be stripped off completely and a fresh polish applied.

Blemishes in French polish. Local treatments. When French polished furniture has been repaired, the new wood may be of a slightly different colour, and will in any case have to be brought to the same kind of polish as the original. Mahogany can be darkened with bichromate of potash applied until the colour is slightly lighter than that of the original, as the French polish will darken it further. When the stained area is dry, apply French polish to the patches, leaving plenty of time for drying between rubs. If the colour is still not right, touch it up with polish containing dry powder pigment as before, and then, when it is drying, put on another rub of French polish to hold it. Some workers like to finish by putting on one complete rub of polish to blend the new work with the old.

Scratches. Proprietary scratch removers can be bought, but it is best to treat individual scratches by abrading them with flour paper dipped in linseed oil, and then put on a rub of dark French polish. Deep scratches can be removed by filling them with coloured beeswax. Make up some melted wax with the appropriate colour, slightly darker than the surrounding surface, and when it has cooled rub it into the scratch; finish with flour paper and then a rub of French polish.

Heat Marks. Left by hot plates or cups or dishes, or by hot water being spilt upon the polished surface, these unsightly marks don't come off very easily. A good rub with equal quantities of linseed oil and real turps may shift them. Or try camphorated oil instead of linseed. Then clean up the oil etc. with vinegar. It may take several treatments before the mark goes. Proprietary ring removers are equally effective.

Spirit Marks. The careless drinker who puts a glass of whisky on to a polished surface and then spills it ought to be banished from highly polished homes, or given beer to drink instead. Spilt spirit is a solvent strong enough to remove French polish or to soften it at any rate. If spirit is spilt it should be wiped up instantly, and the surface left to harden again before it is rubbed or polished. If the polish has come away, however, it will have to be re-polished by painting on the appropriate coloured polish with a small brush until the surface level of the original polish is matched. Then the area is rubbed with flour paper dipped in linseed oil and eventually rubbed hard with a fad until the right polish is achieved.

If either heat or alcohol marks are not too deep, and they are usually quite superficial, a rub with fine steel wool will shift them, but it may be necessary to rub right over the surface of the piece to get an even finish before rewaxing with furniture polish. Cigar ash made into paste will remove some white marks, but unless a member of the family is a cigar smoker this can be an expensive way of doing the job and probably won't be totally effective anyway. Cellulose thinners, applied sparingly on a soft cotton pad and rubbed lightly over the mark, will remove it, but be careful not to wet more surface than is necessary or you will be faced with refinishing big patches.

Cigarette Burns. Depending on how deep the burn is, treatments vary. A very shallow burn can be scraped clean with a blade, or sandpaper or steel wool, and then coloured to match surrounding areas with artist's oil colour smeared in with a finger. Then the area is repolished or sprayed with a clear plastic spray. Deep depressions must be cleaned of all charred wood and then filled. This can be done with coloured wax melted into the hole, or with epoxy resin tinted with dry colour to match, Epoxy resin does not polish well, but is fine where a mirror finish is not required.

Children's wax crayons melted down are fine, but the only varnish which will set over this is shellac.

Black spots. Black marks on furniture, if they are caused by water getting under the finish, can be removed by Oxalic acid. Use a saturated solution made up by adding crystals to a cup of water until no more will dissolve.

Fading. If French polished furniture has been exposed to sunlight, it may have faded, and the underlying wood have become bleached. The surface polish must be removed, preferably with turpentine and methylated spirit. Let the wood dry out and then wash it with a cotton wool swab dipped in dilute vinegar. When this has dried rub a mixture of equal parts of linseed oil and turpentine into the bleached parts, stopping when the colour has reached the right depth. Then put on one layer of French polish and paint in the colours you require with a brush or a cotton wool swab. Make up these colours by adding dry powder pigments to French polish (burnt or raw umber, or burnt sienna, will probably give the right colours).

Let the whole thing dry out for several days before adding a final rub of French polish.

General. It is possible to rub down French polish with fine steel wool, before waxing it, and this makes it resemble a waxed surface, with a nice soft sheen, although it never really has the same depth. Proprietary brands of French polish come in a variety of colours from clear to black so there is no need to make up your own (see page 188).

Wax polishing. There are many proprietary brands of furniture polishes, and many recipes for making one's own.

Wax polish should be applied sparingly to furniture and rubbed until it shines. Frequent applications of wax over the years result in the build up of patina, which no varnish type polish, ancient or modern, can reproduce.

Oak, deal, and beech furniture was traditionally finished by oiling and waxing, or with an oil or turpentine gum based varnish. Veneer and marquetry were never varnished with anything containing turpentine which could soak down and soften the glue, so polishes based on quick drying volatile spirit were used for veneers and for woods such as mahogany which do not readily absorb oil.

For more details of wax polishes, look under *Beeswax*.

Spray finishes. Modern clear spray finishes in aerosols are quite easy to use provided the surface of the work is kept horizontal. Finish by rubbing down with fine steel wool, a little or a lot according to how dull a finish you require, before waxing with furniture polish. If you like a mirror finish, leave the sprayed surface untouched.

Dull finishes. Modern sealers, such as Ronseal, are applied direct to raw wood. They sink in, dry and prevent other lacquers from sinking too far in when they in turn are applied. Thus they make good primers with which to make certain of an even finish with clear lacquers of any type, either painted or sprayed on. Raw wood treated with sealer and then rubbed down, and then polished with furniture polish or beeswax polish, gives a dull sheen which is very attractive.

Linseed oil can be rubbed directly into raw wood, repeating the treatment after several days until the exact degree of darkness is achieved. The grain is heightened by oil, and the wood will polish with beeswax although it will take time and elbow grease to get a good polish.

French polishing. Most of the treatments mentioned above are short cuts or just patching up, and the application of French polish is only touched on briefly. You may want to strip your junk right down and French polish it properly, and there are no short cuts. Good French polishing is a matter of practice, like so many things, but is quite expensive if you get an expert to do the work. Methods vary slightly, but here follows a short description of the techniques.

First make some fads from unbleached wadding. Cut an eight inch square of wadding and soak it in the polish you are going to use and leave it to dry right out. Then soften the fad again with a little meths and squeeze it out. Fold it in half across its width, then fold both sides down triangularly, then fold in both corners of the triangle (see Fig. 20). Mould the fad with your hand into a convenient pear shape. Pour polish on to the fad, but don't make it too wet. Tap the sole of the fad a time or two, on a piece of brown paper, to flatten it and distribute the polish evenly. Rub the fad straight across the wooden surface, backwards and forwards across the grain recharging it with polish when necessary. Don't use oil to lubricate until there are several layers of polish. Be careful not to put too much polish on the fad or it will form ridges on the surface of the work.

After the first coat of polish, rub it all down lightly with glass paper to get rid of any blemishes, surplus filler etc. Do this twice, allowing the coat to harden each time between coats.

Next begin to build up the polish. Recharge the fad and shake a few drops of white mineral oil on to the surface to be polished. Change to a circular motion and work away. You can see by the oily smear when you have covered the whole surface. Let it harden, and rub down with the finest glass paper if there are any specks of dust.

Now for the rubbing. First make a new fad and charge it with polish from the back. Cover it with a cloth—an old handkerchief is perfect. Cut a piece eight inches square and fold it carefully so that the face of the rubber is quite flat, don't just pull the cloth into a bunch at the back as this will distort the shape of the fad. Charge the rubber, and put a few drops of oil on the work and rub with a figure-of-eight motion. Put on a drop more oil, and a fresh cover on the fad, recharge it, and rub again backwards and forwards. Leave the surface to harden right off.

Now comes the process known as bodying, which is the building up of the exact thickness of clear shellac that you require. French polish is, of course, shellac dissolved in methylated spirit, with a little oil and perhaps some colouring matter. The meths and oil allow the shellac to be spread across the surface, the spirit evaporates away leaving a coat of shellac, and the oil, used solely as a lubricant is finally polished away. Therefore, as you rub polish on and the spirit evaporates, don't rub too hard or the shellac will become a sticky, tacky, ridged mess. This is where the art and experience come in. The only way to judge if the pressure being applied is right is by the pull on the rubber, and when the pull becomes too great then drops of oil are added.

Charge the rubber so that a little polish appears when the sole is pressed, but not so much that it drips. Work in large circles until the whole surface has been covered, increasing pressure slightly as the polish is used up. Let the rubber get almost dry before recharging. Then change to a figure-of-eight movement, then into an all over circular movement, and finish with up-and-down movements. Finally, make up a new rubber and go right over the surface, but without using oil and with a very light charge of polish. This should remove all the oil. If the surface, looked at with light across it, shows oil smears, put a new cloth on the rubber and go over it again, very lightly. Let the polish harden right off. If you want an even thicker coat of shellac, rub down with flour paper with oil on it, very lightly, and continue with another bodying coat. When you have repeated this one or more times to your satisfaction, leave the oil on the last bodying coat and proceed with finishing.

Immediately after the last bodying coat, charge a fresh rubber with a little polish and a little methylated spirit, and rub again with small circular movements, then in large circular movements, and then up and down. Finally, make a rubber up with a clean cloth and a clean piece of fine linen. Sprinkle a little meths in your hand and charge the rubber with this. Hold the rubber to your lips and if it feels wet, there is too much meths on it. It should feel slightly cold. Rub it up and down until the surface is bright and quite free from oil.

All this sounds very complicated, but it is a matter of care, elbow grease and, above all, practice. Make sure that all oil is rubbed away at the end of each stage so that none becomes trapped in the polish, work in a dry atmosphere, as damp causes bloom, and don't overcharge the fad or rubber at any stage.

French polish can be bought in various colours.

White: Milky coloured for use on light wood only.

Transparent: Quite clear, so keeps the natural colour of the wood.

Button: Slightly opaque yellow, do not put on over dark wood, stain, or dark polish.

Orange: Golden Brown.

Garnet: Dark Brown.

Black: For use on ebonised wood.

Coloured polish: For matching and tinting. If you add

spirit soluble aniline dyes to white, transparent, or orange polish, various colours can be obtained.

Antiqueing Furniture

One method of antiqueing is described in the section on *Picture Framing* but there is a way of treating old furniture which differs a little from this and which can be very attractive indeed if it is well done.

Basically the technique is to apply a coat of a light colour, usually green, blue or white, ochre, or cream or grey. The ground coat may be glossy or flat; personally I prefer the flat paint as it looks older. The paint is put on quite roughly as you are not trying to achieve a factory finish. Any decoration is then applied; and most expert antiquers do paint designs on their furniture, either with white paint, and a darker tone of the ground colour, or by using gold transfer foil (see *Gilding*) for gilt decorations. Knobs or strips or borders are sometimes painted in—it is a matter of personal taste. Then a coat of glaze, or varnish tinted with burnt umber, or raw umber, or black, or white, is put on along the edges and corners, and wiped outwards with a rag towards the centres of the surfaces. A little rottenstone or pumice powder mixed with water to make a paint is brushed along edges or anywhere where dust is likely to lodge. When all is dry give the whole thing a rub over with fine steel wool, and then wax polish, and you have a piece of genuine (!) antique painted furniture. Those who do this job professionally are loath to part with their secrets, each having his own favourite ingredient to add to the glaze or paint to give it the look of faded age. Some antiquers put on several ground coats on top of each other, rubbed down unevenly to show colour through.

Mending Furniture

As a general rule, do just as little dismantling and repair as is strictly necessary. A lot can be done by cleaning and re-glueing joints, by removing old screws and nails and replacing them with wooden dowels or new screws. Mortices and tenons often need repair, and mouldings have missing parts which need replacing. Put in whole or part new pieces where necessary. How much you can do rather depends upon how well equipped your workshop is. Cramps of all shapes and sizes are essential, and it is important to study the principles of cramping and applying pressure to repairs without damaging the wood or the piece of furniture as a whole. As in china repair, it is essential to apply pressure to stuck joints.

Build up a stock of pieces of old sound wood, even buy junk which is well past repair in order to get one or two pieces of sound wood. It is so much easier to match up with old wood than with new. Broken veneers can be replaced and marquetry mended, quite successfully, especially if you have a stock of old pieces to use for patching.

Chests of drawers. Chests of drawers which have been painted or varnished can be stripped down to the natural wood and simply waxed or repolished. It is simple to make new handles to replace ugly Victorian knobs, or to fix brass handles. To make new drawer handles, cut blocks of any suitable wood (see Fig. 21b), with a slight inward slope to give a better grip. Cut short pegs from dowelling of the same size as the holes left by the old knobs, and bore holes half way through the new handles from the insides and set the pegs into them. When the glue has set, put impact adhesive on the inside faces of the handles and on the

Fig. 21a

drawer fronts, and push the handles into place. If brass handles are to be put on the chest, then the old knob holes must be pegged with a short piece of dowel and the wood stained or polished to match, before the new handles are screwed on.

If drawers do not slide well, check that the various surfaces are clean and free from obstruction, and rub sliding parts with candle grease. If the drawer joints are loose, dismantle the drawer and re-glue it. The joints will probably be dovetailed. Remove the drawer bottom (which may also need repair or replacement), by taking

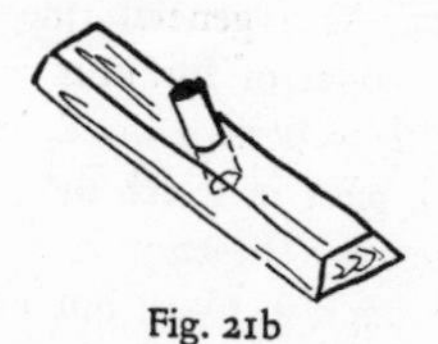

Fig. 21b

out the screws which hold it in place, and sliding it out of its grooves. Then tap the joints apart. Never, when dismantling furniture, just bang it with a hammer, always use a spare piece of wood as a cushion and hammer this, so avoiding damage to the furniture by splitting it or bruising it with the hammer head. Scrape off old glue and tidy the joins with sandpaper. Any really bad pieces will have to be renewed. Use the old bits as a pattern for cutting new pieces. Reglue the joints and tap them together again. As joints are dovetailed, cramping should not be necessary. Always check to see that the drawer is square, using a try square, and then leave it until the glue is set.

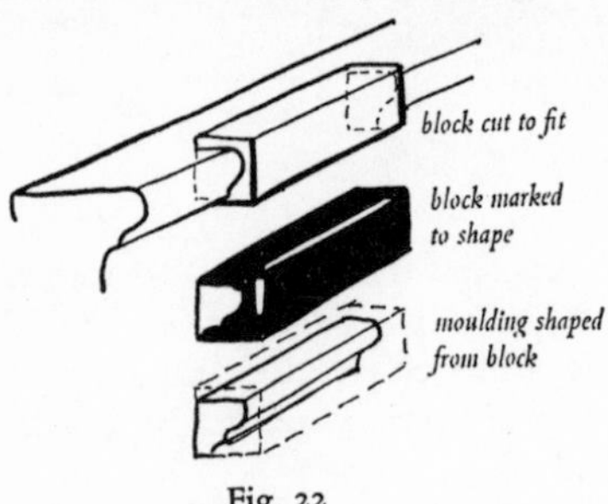

Fig. 22

The drawer bottom, if worn, cracked or shrunk, can best be replaced with plywood. In the old days, drawer bottoms were usually in two or three strips, only because wider pieces were not obtainable.

Broken Mouldings. As a general rule, when mouldings, or pieces of the edges of furniture are broken, cut the damaged part back to perfect wood, and then replace the piece with a fresh piece in which the grain runs as exactly as possible in the same direction as it did in the original. Small pieces are stuck in place, but where there is likely to be a lot of wear, it is best to peg the piece in if possible, or to cut some kind of rebate to help hold it. Cut a piece and fit it to the hole, without at first attempting to shape the moulding however simple. When you have tailored the block to fit, mark the shape of the moulding on the end of it, and then shape it properly. When you are satisfied that it is a perfect match (see Fig. 22), fix it into position. Final sanding and shaping can be done after the adhesive has set. Apply stain, if any is necessary, before doing any refixing.

Loose Tenons. You may find that a piece of furniture has been repaired with an iron plate or bracket, especially where a mortice and tenon joint has disintegrated. The metal plate may be effective, but it is a clumsy way to mend wood, and provided the main member is sound, the mortice and tenon can be remade.

Remove the iron plate and the piece with the broken tenon. Examine the mortice and clean it out. If any part of the mortice is broken away, cut back to sound wood, and make a replacement piece and glue it in. Then cut away the broken tenon altogether, and cut a new one from a fresh piece of wood, making it an exact fit in the mortice, but twice the length. Then cut a slot in the other piece to take the new tenon. Now you can either glue the tenon into its slot, running a dowel through if necessary to strengthen the mend, and then replace it in the mortice in the normal way, glueing the whole thing together and cramping it; or you can glue it into the mortice first, and then put

Fig. 23

the tenon section on, glueing and pegging as necessary (see Fig. 23).

If you wish to renew a mortice tenon joint, but don't want to take several sound joins apart just to get at one broken one, try getting a loose tenon into position. Clean out the mortice, and cut away the old tenon (see Fig. 24). Make a slot in the tenon side opposite the mortice, but

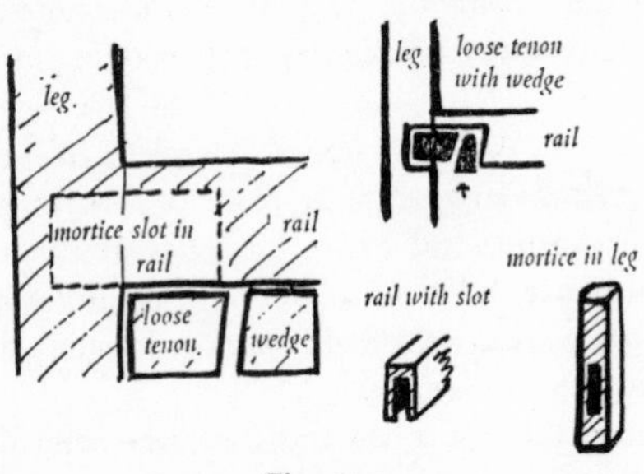

Fig. 24

longer than the mortice slot. Cut a loose tenon the same size as the tenon slot, with a sloping end. Push this piece up into the tenon slot, then move it sideways into the mortice. It should enter the mortice and go right home, part of it still protruding into the tenon slot. Then cut a wedge and bang it into the gap to make everything tight. If all the surfaces have been glued before the final assembly, and the whole is cramped and left to set, a good strong joint wil result. Dowels can be run through to strengthen the joints.

Cramping. Cramping is a bit of an art and it is so important. Big and small cramps, corner cramps, thumb screws etc. are all invaluable tools for the furniture restorer. Cut upholstery springs make useful cramps for small items, and in some cases, pieces of stout cord used in the same way as a tourniquet, can be got round a mend where no cramp will fit. Cut blocks of wood to fit curves, on which the flat faced cramp will bear. No cramp should ever be screwed direct to wood without a block cushion of some sort. Firstly the block prevents bruising of the wood, secondly it spreads the pressure of the cramp so that it is effective over a wider area.

Dowelling. Dowelling is one of the simplest and best ways to strengthen joints and to repair old furniture. Broken dowels can easily be tapped or drilled out and replaced by new dowels, and old screws and nails can be replaced in the same way. Hardwood dowelling can be bought in various sizes at handyman shops, or you can make pegs out of odds and ends. A dowel should fit tightly but not so tightly that it has to be hammered home, thus risking splitting the piece you are trying to mend. If a dowel only goes part of the way through the wood, cut into the dowel hole with a fine saw blade or flatten one side of the dowel to let air that is trapped beneath it escape as it is tapped home, together with any surplus glue.

Missing parts. Table legs, chair legs, arms etc. may be missing or broken so that large sections must be replaced. As furniture is more or less symmetrical, it is usually possible to take measurements from another arm or leg and make a copy. To replace half a piece is not quite so easy. Small end pieces of legs etc. can be cut square and dowelled and stuck into place, but larger sections which will have to bear weight, must be spliced (see Fig. 25). Central, square splices, parallel with the edges of the piece being mended, are not particularly strong, and if possible make a tapered splice. Try to make the joins run in the direction of the grain. Tapered joins have wider bases or

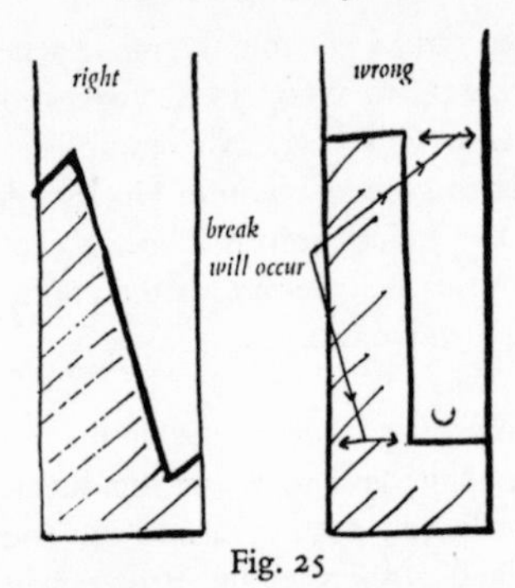

Fig. 25

roots, and are less likely to snap than square splices. Dowel the splices into position, or if screws are used, counterbore the holes and put in wooden pellets so that the screw heads are not visible.

Knuckle and Finger Hinges. Pivoting legs on tables, or pivoting flaps which hold up the leaves, frequently become worn or break. If it is the knuckle or finger on the table section which has broken away, cut a new block to fit, and stick and dowel it into position, first having removed the pin which runs through the whole hinge! Reassemble the hinge and replace the pin. If the knuckle on the leg or flap is broken, repair it in the same way, or make a new flap section.

The tightness of this type of hinge is governed by the close fit of the knuckle surfaces, which should bear exactly on each other without binding and without play. If the hinge has become loose through wear, tighten up the hinge by removing the flap section and sticking veneer on each of the bearing surfaces. Sand down the surfaces until the fit is perfect, and then reassemble the hinge. If the pinhole itself has got too big, just put in a thicker pin!

Cracks. Cracks in panels which run along the grain of the wood are usually caused by stress, and to put glue in and cramp the crack edges together again will only make a temporary repair, for the same stresses still exist and will in time open the crack again or make another one. The best method is to cut a sliver of wood and glue it into the crack, smoothing down well when the adhesive has set, and staining and polishing till the new pieces blend in with the old.

Warped panels. Such things as table tops occasionally warp, and to bring the wood back level again is not easy. If the top is in sections, then the boards can be parted and the edges planed so that when reassembled the whole thing lies flat. A strong batten can be screwed across the underside of a warped panel, but this is obviously not practicable where the batten will show and look clumsy. Sometimes a table top can be cramped back to its proper level shape and screwed down to the top rails of the table.

Metal Hinges. Hinges are frequent trouble spots especially on items like desks or bureaux with fall fronts, because the flaps get opened without the side supports being pulled out, and allowed to drop, thus straining the hinges. Where the screw holes in either part have got to the state where they don't hold screws, but the piece is otherwise undamaged, take the hinges off completely, and make pegs to fill the screw holes. Stick the pegs firmly into place with Aerolite glue. When the glue has set, screw the hinges back into place again exactly as if they were being put into new wood, with guide holes bored for the screws. If the wood surrounding the screwholes is chipped or broken, cut out the whole section and replace it with a matching piece of wood spliced, glued and dowelled into place. Then replace the hinges. This kind of repair is suitable for any kind of metal hingeing where loose screws and wood breakage are the problem.

It may be that the cause of the loosening of the screws or breakage of the wood in the first place was some binding or misfitting of the hinge which has put a strain or pull on to it. Perhaps the screw heads are so big that they have not gone down into the countersinking but have remained proud so that the door or flap will not shut properly unless force is applied which in turn pulls the screws. The remedy is obvious, either to deepen the countersinking, or to plug the screwhole as above so that smaller screws can be used.

The recesses in which a hinge is set may be too deep, which also causes binding and pulling and consequent screw loosening. The remedy is to pack out the recesses with pieces of veneer behind the hinge.

If hinges are binding or pulling because of shrinkage, swelling, or warping of the carcase of the furniture, the cure is to tackle the problem at its source and to correct the faults in the piece if possible. Otherwise the hinges may have to be packed out or reset, or parts of the furniture filed or planed back to remove the cause of the binding.

Veneer. Blisters on veneer can be laid by cutting with a razor blade or a scalpel. Scotch glue is slid underneath with a palette knife, and the veneer pressed back into place. Cover the area with greaseproof paper and put a heavy weight on top until you are certain the glue must be set. Scotch glue is excellent for veneer work.

Save old pieces of veneer, they are invaluable for repair work. As they were always put in place with animal glues they can be soaked or steamed off, and cleaned, and even quite small pieces have their uses. In order to lift veneer, heat a soldering iron and place a damp cloth on the area to be raised, then use the iron carefully to make plenty of steam so that the glue will eventually melt and the piece will lift off. Use an ordinary iron for big areas. A domestic steam iron over a cloth is fine, provided the area stays damp the whole time. Damp cannot penetrate polish, so make sure you have cleaned off all old polish, varnish or wax before trying to lift veneer. Clean off any old glue on the veneer and on the main body of the piece. If the veneer has buckled, damp it and flatten it between two well warmed blocks of wood, or 'cauls' and cramp it together and leave it to dry—but be sure there is no glue left anywhere or the veneer will stick to the cauls.

The edges of veneered furniture get chipped very easily, and the pieces are usually lost up a vacuum cleaner! The older the veneer, the thicker it is, because old veneer was saw cut. Modern veneer is knife cut and is thinner. Cut pieces from a block of wood with a saw to get thick replacement pieces, or build up two or three layers of thin veneer.

To replace a chipped piece of veneer cut back carefully to a straight working edge (see Fig. 26) preferably along the grain or diagonally across it. Then find a matching piece, with the grain running the same way. Take a piece of paper and place it on the part to be mended and rub it over with a piece of heel ball, or a soft lead pencil, to get an outline of the patch on the paper exactly as one takes brass rubbings, or once made the pattern of the face of a penny. Cut the paper roughly to the pattern and stick it on to your piece of repair veneer, making sure that the grain runs the right way. Next cut out the shape, very slightly larger than the pattern mark, with a fretsaw. The more skilled you become, the more exactly you can cut your patch, but it is safer to cut the patch a little large and then sand it down

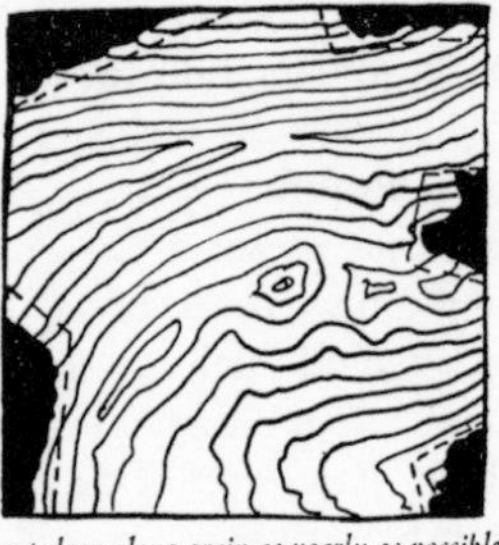

cut clean along grain as nearly as possible

Fig. 26

rather than to cut it too small and have to start all over again. Keep the paper stuck on until the veneer patch is quite ready to stick in place as it helps to keep it rigid and avoids cracking, while sanding or filing to fit. When all is ready, peel off the paper and glue the veneer patch into place. Put a piece of greaseproof paper over the top and lay a heavy weight on it, or cramp a flat piece of warmed wood over it. The important thing is to get the veneer down really tight, without any air bubbles being trapped underneath. When it is set in hard, sandpaper it down exactly to the surface level of the surrounding wood. Always have your veneer patch a little thicker than it need be so that there is some latitude for sanding, and also that any clamping or weighting will bear hard on the new patch and not on the old wood.

Inlaid veneer bands often come adrift, and it is difficult to find matching woods with which to replace them. Bands of inlay can be made up quite easily (see Fig. 27), and as they are always thick cut, can be sliced with a circular saw on a power drill. Inlay bands are usually cross grained, so the wood must be cut from the end grain of blocks of like wood glued side by side. Cut your blocks from one piece if possible, all in the same thickness, which should be two veneer thicknesses less than the groove to be filled, to accommodate the veneer edging of the band. Lay the blocks side by side on a piece of newspaper spread on a flat surface and glue them together and cramp tight. When set, plane the surfaces level. Next stick a flat piece of veneer to each side to the block and cramp it flat. When the whole is set, the banding strips can be sliced off the ends as required. This banding will go round slight curves, but for tight curves pieces will have to be cut in small fan shapes and fitted.

Marquetry. Replacing or repairing marquetry, which is veneer inlaid into furniture in patterns, is a little more difficult. Damp may have lifted the inlay, letting dust and dirt creep underneath. In such cases remove the whole surface using the damp cloth and hot iron method described above. Clean the base and the veneer and restick into position. Gummed strip will hold the veneer pieces in place while the glue dries, but the piece should be weighted as well.

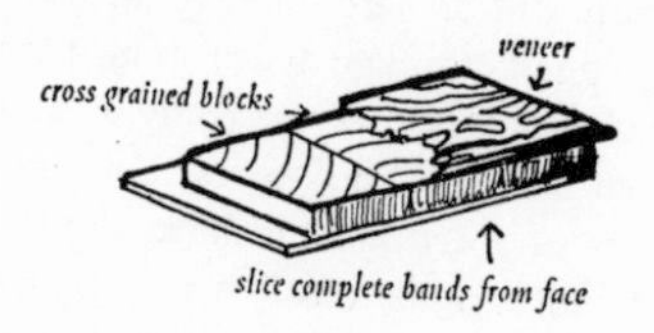

Fig. 27

If the marquetry is not too badly lifted try pressing it down with a warmed caul and cramping it well. The warmth melts the old glue slightly and if the marquetry is pressed well down it may stick back into position without further trouble.

If a piece of marquetry is missing, take a pattern with paper and heel ball as described above and cut a new piece with a sharp knife or a fret saw. Matching is always a difficulty, and this is where a good stock of oddments comes in handy. Press the piece into place, after cleaning the base and reglueing, with the rounded end of a ball peen hammer used rather like a squeegee, taking care not to roughen the grain by working across it too heavily.

Very small missing pieces can be replaced by coloured wax, melted in and smoothed down.

Use Scotch glue or Evostik 528 for veneers.

Stripping Down

Traditionally, while the hardwoods were left in their natural state and polished in various ways, but never painted, softwood furniture was always painted. In this country many people believe that soft woods are ugly to look at and must be painted. Anyone who has been to a part of the world where many pine trees grow knows that soft woods look just as beautiful as hardwoods if they are properly finished. The biggest problem when using new softwood in this country is that it is rarely perfectly seasoned and will shrink and warp and spoil good work. However, there are many old pieces of softwood furniture about covered in layers of paint and varnish, and it is astonishing what can be made of them by stripping them right off, making good damage, and filling where necessary, and then finishing with wax, or oil, or with modern glazes, either left bright or sanded down for a matt finish.

I have an old pine corner cupboard, and a pine chest of drawers (see Fig. 21) which were both hideous and covered in layers of paint. The chest of drawers had bulbous legs and round knobs, and with these removed and new strip handles put on the drawers, it looks much more in keeping with modern decor. The wood itself was cleaned of all paint, and just waxed with furniture polish.

Paint can be stripped from furniture in various ways; by using proprietary paint stripper, or caustic soda, or ammonia or trisodium phosphate, with scrapers and steel wool; or by working directly with sanding discs on a power drill.

To strip down with a power sander takes practice with the tool and delicacy of touch. It is easy enough on softwood furniture with flat surfaces, and which is fairly rugged. A mistake causes nasty semicircular cuts deep into the wood which cannot be removed without leaving a long dimple in the surface. I have successfully sanded down soft wood pieces, and taken off a lot of the old paint and varnish from all kinds of surfaces, leaving difficult and rounded parts to be done by hand. The power tool does save time. Use fairly coarse carbide spaced grit discs to start with and finish with the finest discs. Paint clogs the discs but this can be cleared with a wire brush. You will use a lot of discs, which can make this method quite expensive.

Paint stripper is also expensive, but it is effective on most paints and varnishes. Put it on with an old brush, and leave it for a few minutes to lift the paint, and then remove it with scrapers. Skarstens make scrapers which have blades in all shapes and sizes and are wonderful stripping tools. They must be kept sharp, and careless use can cause damage by scoring. Steel wool, especially in the form of pads, is useful in conjunction with the paint stripper.

Caustic soda, used in the open air on a warm day (it won't work in cold weather), while wearing rubber gloves and overalls, is an excellent paint stripper. Use one can of caustic soda to one quart of water. Mix them in a bucket, always putting the water in the bucket first and adding the crystals to it, or there will be a lot of dangerous spitting. Soak the paint thoroughly with the liquid, using a small mop of some kind. Keep applying it and rubbing with the mop until all the paint is dissolved. Use a wire brush and a knife or scraper to get paint out of odd corners. Wash the paint and caustic off with a hose or several buckets of clean water sloshed all over the furniture. Wipe the piece dry and give it a final swab down with vinegar. Caustic soda darkens wood, but this can be put right by using domestic bleach instead of vinegar for the final wipe.

Ammonia may shift old paint that caustic won't touch. Use it straight out of the bottle and rub it on with steel wool. Rinse well. Ammonia also darkens wood and you may wish to bleach as before.

On the other hand, clear varnish or glaze can be applied direct on to ammonia-cleaned wood, provided it has dried out well, and you will be saved the cost of a tin of stain.

Trisodium phosphate, which is an active ingredient in some detergents, will also remove paint. It is used as a saturated solution in hot water. It must be handled with care, but is not so liable to burn as caustic soda. Wear rubber gloves, though. This chemical doesn't darken wood very much, and in any case bleaching can follow.

All these methods which entail drenching the furniture with water and chemicals have their disadvantages. Wood swells when it gets wet, and animal glue melts in hot water. Bearing this in mind, these methods are probably cheaper than using sanding discs or paint stripper if you have a lot of work to do.

Remember also that stripping down, whichever way it is done, makes a terrible mess, either in the form of paint dust, or slimy strippings. I find it necessary to tie a handkerchief or a piece of gauze round my nose and mouth while sanding.

When using a power sander indoors is unavoidable, run a vacuum cleaner with the intake as near as possible to the sanding point. Quite a lot of the dust will be drawn into the cleaner.

FURS, TIGER SKINS ETC.

If you do have anything of this kind which you wish to restore, it would obviously be best, if the fur is at all valuable, to pay an expert furrier to cope with it. However, it may be helpful to know how to clean up furs. Dark furs can be cleaned with dry bran heated on a tray to 250 deg. F. for three-quarters of an hour. The hot bran is immediately rubbed into the fur. Cover with a piece of old blanket, which has been warmed up on a radiator, leave for half an hour and then shake the bran out and brush the fur. Light coloured furs can be treated by being rubbed well with cornflour. Cover with a hot blanket, roll up into a sausage and leave overnight before shaking and brushing out.

Stains can be cleaned with carbon tetrachloride but this must not come into contact with the leather hide or skin, only with the hair. When the stain has shifted, air the fur well, and give it a good brush.

Fuller's Earth, rubbed well into a fur is always a useful cleaning material.

GARDEN SEATS, PEWS ETC.

It is sometimes possible to pick up those old park or garden seats with iron frames and wooden slats, in reasonable condition. If the cast iron parts are broken they are extremely difficult to mend except by bolting linking plates through ornamental parts. The type which has three ornamental cast iron legs makes into good garden furniture, especially if you can get hold of a pair, which means you then have six legs, and can make three two legged shorter seats. If the wood of the old slats feels sound when probed with a pen-knife, it might be worthwhile stripping off the layers of old paint, and repainting from scratch either with a good coat of primer, undercoat and topcoat, or with polyurethane varnish. The metal legs should be scrubbed down with a wire brush and paint or rust remover, until they are clean, and then repainted. Basically the treatment for any items of this kind is to clean thoroughly, to mend or replace broken parts, and then to cover with good weather-resistant paints or varnishes.

Old pine chapel pews make good garden seats and I once came across a junk shop selling a job lot of these off very cheaply. Some repairs were needed where the pews had been roughly dismantled. The old varnish was stripped off, and the seat was revarnished with several coats of polyurethane yacht varnish.

GESSO

Gesso is a mixture of glue and plaster, used to make a priming layer. Canvases may be primed with gesso, furniture may have a layer to take gilding, and picture frames very often have a gesso layer on which the gilding is set. It is made from whiting, chalk, kaolin, or gypsum mixed with glue, or gelatine or casein, and sometimes it has white pigment in it.

When making up gesso to do restoration jobs, add a little four per cent formalin solution to act as a preservative. The mixture is made fairly thin so that it can be painted on and usually several coats are applied to get a good surface. Once it has dried gesso does not expand, and although it was frequently used to prime canvas, it is not entirely satisfactory as it may crack badly in time, due to its lack of flexibility. On solid panels of any kind it is an excellent primer and hence its common use on furniture and on picture frames.

Gesso can be bought in tins.

GILDING

Junk objects which need regilding always present quite a problem, for to do the job really perfectly using gold leaf is expert work, which takes a lot of experience of handling the rather difficult materials involved. On the other hand, gilt paints can be very harsh and not at all satisfactory. Nevertheless, there are a lot of new gilding materials on the market which will do the job without leaving the piece with that brazen glare of a radiator in a public building!

I think that one of the techniques of using gold leaf should first be described, as in some cases it could be really necessary and you might decide to chance your arm rather than send the piece to a professional gilder. The room in which the gilding is done should be as dust free as possible, with no draughts, and should be kept at a warm, even temperature. First clean the object to be gilded with a weak solution of ammonia, taking great care to keep things as dry as possible, so as to avoid any swelling of underlying wood, loosening of glues, or drops of moisture remaining to spoil the work. When the object has dried right out and you are satisfied that it is quite clean, apply a coat of gold size, and leave this until the degree of tackiness is hardly perceptible. The trick in gilding is to judge this degree of tackiness, for if the size is too wet the gold leaf will wrinkle when applied, and if it is too dry, it will not stick properly. Experience alone will teach you to judge this.

Gold leaf is bought in books of twenty-five sheets interleaved with tissue paper, and it is so thin that a sigh of despair can send leaves floating across the room. The separate leaves are placed on the size, slightly overlapping, all in one direction, and any gaps are filled with scraps of leaf. When the cover is complete, it is very carefully rubbed in the direction of the overlaps with a clean cotton cloth until all is blended together to form an even finish. That is a brief description of the simplest of the gold leaf gilding techniques, but I do advise that any really valuable pieces should be taken to an expert.

Gold leaf can be bought from art shops. Illuminating Gold leaf is prepared from 24 carat gold and is therefore the richest in colour. Best English Gold Leaf is the type used for tooling on books. Transfer Gold Leaf is much the most convenient form to use since each leaf has a thin paper tissue on the front which enables the gold to be handled more easily. Once the leaf is in position the tissue is separated from the gold. Gold leaf is normally fixed to paper or vellum by means of Water Matt Gold Size, and to wood by Japan Gold Size. For textiles, Wintex Fabric Painting Yellow or Saree Relief Yellow which has been allowed to dry to a tacky state may be used as an adhesive. Genuine silver was sometimes used for illumination in the past but it is not really suitable as it blackens with age. For a permanent silver colour, use aluminium or platinum foil. Both are supplied in the same form as gold leaf, but platinum leaf is very much more expensive, a single leaf costing as much as a complete book of aluminium. All these items of leaf mentioned here are supplied by Winsor & Newton, and can be purchased from artist's supply shops.

A far simpler method of regilding, which is suitable for many things, is to rub on colour with a piece of cloth or your finger. The advantage of this method is that if it is done carefully a very soft effect can be achieved. Reeves make a gold paste called Restoration Wax, which comes in Bright Gold, Yellow Gold or Copper Gold, and also in Silver; Winsor & Newton supply through art shops an American make of metallic paste known as Treasure Wax. This comes in a whole series of colours, all of which have their uses, depending on the type of surface on which they are to be applied. All these waxes are applied with a finger, and can be buffed to a fine lustre. They are virtually non-tarnishing because of their wax content, and dry very quickly sticking pretty well to most surfaces. However, if it is intended to clean the objects with metal polish the colour may come away. It is best to varnish over the wax of an object which would otherwise be polished. Winsor & Newton's Colour Varnish, based on alcohol, will seal in the wax without lifting any of the underlying colour. Don't use varnishes which contain turpentine or white spirit as they will lift the wax. The wax adheres to wood, metal, plaster or plastic. It has many uses for both complete regilding and for antiqueing and touching up odd spots. I have found it most useful for regilding the gilt linings of picture frames. It is quite expensive, but each pot goes a very long way, and it is the most durable and accurate substitute for genuine gold leaf that I know.

Metallic brushing paints can be made by mixing colours with these wax pastes. Treasure Silver should be thinned with turpentine and mixed into flat black, and this makes a gunmetal colour for use on indoor or outdoor statuary. Treasure Copper or Treasure Renaissance and flat black make a dark bronze. Any of these wax gilts can be removed in turpentine.

Treasure Liquid Leaf is also an American product, but can be bought in this country, in 1 oz. bottles. It is particularly suitable for decorating plain or carved picture frames, ceramic figures, ornamental metals and furniture. Brush on a single coat only. Apply Liquid Leaf to flat surfaces such as leather or glass, with a pen. Use turpentine or white spirit to clean the tools. Liquid Leaf is obtainable in a large range of metallic colours.

Meltonian make gold and silver aerosol lacquers for gilding leather, and these can be used quite successfully, provided careful masking off of areas surrounding the area to be gilded is carried out. This can be done by making paper masks, or more simply, by carefully covering all the parts in vaseline, except those to be gilded. The gilt spray cannot reach the wrong places, and can be wiped away when the gilded section has dried.

GLASS CUTTING

Glass cutting (see Fig. 28) is one of those rather frightening jobs which the experts make look so easy. I am always fascinated by the panache with which my glass merchant marks out great sheets of glass and snaps them perfectly. But with a little practice it really isn't too hard, and it does save throwing away those broken pieces which can still be cut down for smaller pictures.

It is essential to have a perfectly level smooth table on which to work. It is not recommended that you use the best dining room table unless it has a good cloth upon it. A sheet of hardboard which is perfectly smooth and level, does very well, provided it is itself resting on a table.

You need a long ruler and a straightedge, without a bevel, or a large T square. Put some Sellotape on its underside to prevent the straightedge slipping as you cut. Tap brads into the hardboard (but not the dining room table), to hold the straightedge in position while you work. The glass cutter should always be kept in a pot of turpentine, as it not only prevents rust, but actually helps the glass cutting operation.

Put your piece of glass on the clean table. Lay the straightedge or T square across it as you wish to cut, and then put your ruler at right angles across this and measure off the exact length. Measure at several points down the straightedge to be sure it is square across the glass. The

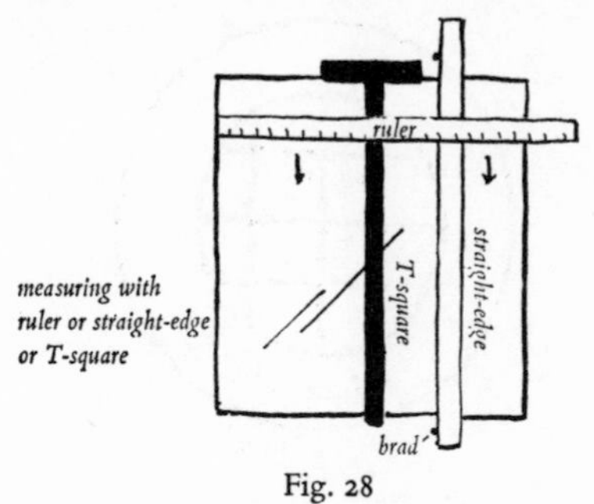

Fig. 28

wheel of the glass cutter is about $\frac{1}{8}''$ from the bearing surface of the cutter, so this much must be deducted from the total measurement. In other words if you wish to cut a piece with a measurement of 10″, measure $9\frac{7}{8}''$ from the edge of the glass to the edge of the straightedge. Then put the brads in if necessary to hold the straightedge in position (see Fig. 28), although with practice, the pressure of the spread fingers will be sufficient. Hold the cutter as if it were a pencil, but firmly. Start your cut at the furthermost edge, but don't start outside it, or you will chip the glass. Draw the cutter across with a firm even stroke until it slides clean off the near edge.

Lift the glass carefully by the largest piece, and tap gently at each end of the cut with the cutter handle. Tap underneath the glass at the outside of the cut, and the glass should split. Then the offcut part can be grasped and parted from the whole. The expert parts the glass by bringing the 'started' sheet to the exact edge of his table, with the waste side outside, and then bearing down smartly on it. It is all a knack which doesn't take long to learn. Practice with waste glass is the best way to learn it.

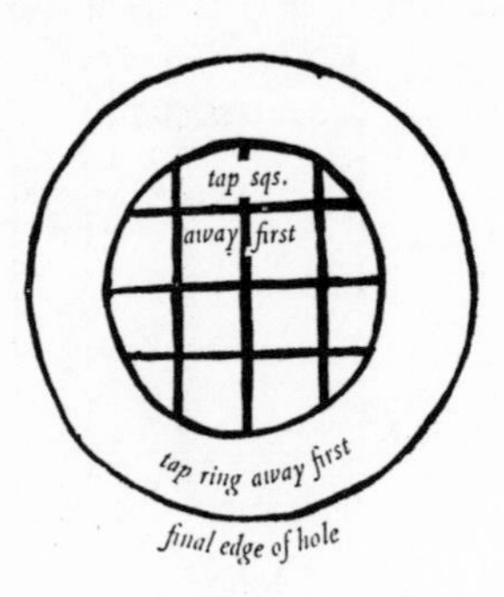

Fig. 29

Circular or curved cuts can be made in the same way but obviously must be drawn freehand, which is a little more difficult. Make a pattern by drawing your outline on a piece of white paper and then lay the glass on it and trace the pattern with the cutter. When cutting circular holes, in order to minimise the risk of breaking the pane and to make sure of a good clean edge, work as follows: Make a second circular score about one inch inside the first ring. Then take an old cutter with which you don't mind criss-crossing score lines, and score the inner ring both ways so that you make a checkerboard pattern of squares, each square having sides of about one inch. Then tap out these squares with the handle of the cutter, and finally tap out the ring (see Fig. 29).

Never score a line twice, or cross a scored line (except with an old cutter). The glass won't break cleanly, and the cutter will be ruined.

The older the glass, the more careful you have to be, as glass becomes brittle. Oil the cutter with turpentine for smoother cutting.

GREASE STAINS

Grease or fat stains are made by any number of things from lubricating oil to cream and must be tackled with appropriate solvents. Grease, if it is left on, collects dust and dirt, so should be removed as soon as possible. Old objects, whatever they are, usually have a certain amount of grease on them even if it is only surface film, for fat particles float around in the atmosphere and cling where they fall. Fingers deposit grease, food gets spilt all over things, and almost all of it contains grease.

Grease marks on glass, china, and porcelain can usually be removed by washing with soap and water or detergent and water, and solutions of ammonia remove grease by turning it into soluble soap. Various solvents, pyridine, petrol and benzine, remove grease (specially suitable for paper). Carbon tetrachloride and proprietary cleaning fluids (Thawpit, Dabitoff etc.) work well on textiles, and grease spots can be removed from stone such as marble by making a paste of kaolin and benzine and overlaying the spot with the paste and allowing it to dry. The solvent sinks into the grease spot and loosens it, the kaolin dries out and draws the solvent back into itself complete with the grease.

Some grease spots can be removed by putting brown paper on them and then ironing. The warm iron draws the grease up into the paper.

For further information on removing grease from particular objects, look under the section for that particular item.

INK STAINS

Ink stains are to be found only too frequently on junk, but in these days of the ubiquitous ball-point, are less and less of a problem. The removal of ink stains rather depends upon the substance which is stained. So often not only is the ink stain removed, but colour, varnish and patina with it.

You can buy two solution ink removers for fabrics and paper, but if you wish to make up your own, try a solution of a quarter of a teaspoonful of oxalic acid to a quarter of a pint of warm water. Apply it to the material, wash it away with clean water, and blot it dry with white blotting paper.

Some inks will not yield to this treatment. Try 1 part of citric acid, 2 parts concentrated solution of borax and 10 parts of distilled water.

Ink stains on some fabrics can be moved by using salts of lemon—this is an equal mixture of cream of tartar and citric acid. Put the stained part of the fabric in a shallow dish of water and rub on the paste until the stain goes.

Glycerine put on a stain and washed off after a while with detergent and water may work.

Milton will remove stains but should be washed out as soon as it has worked. It is a bleach and may bring other colour with it.

Oxalic acid solution may also work on wooden surfaces but usually the stain must be sanded out and the surface repolished.

Chloride of lime made into a paste with water will remove ink stains from silver such as old inkstands.

INSECTS

Silver fish. Silver fish are unpleasant little insects which get their name from the fact that to the naked eye they look just like little tiny silver fish wriggling along. They are particularly destructive to paper, and books, prints, drawings etc. are their favourite food. They like moulds on rotting glues and pastes, especially if they are damp and cool, and this is an exact description of an uncared-for book.

Paradichlorbenzine or carbon disulphide can be used to fumigate articles infested with silverfish and will effectively destroy them. Place the article in an airtight box and surround it with cotton wool impregnated with the vermifuge. Repeat all treatments after a few weeks to destroy any later hatching insects. Either will kill many of the insects which attack books, and Insectrol made by Rentokil in an aerosol container is a very good and easy way of dealing with most of these small insects.

Firebrat. An insect not unlike a silver fish but hardier, which likes dirty old books provided they are warm and dry. It can be destroyed with Paradichlorbenzine or carbon disulphide or Insectrol.

Booklice. Booklice won't eat the paper parts of books but will eat the bindings and will succumb to the same treatment as the insects above.

Clothes Moth. So well known and so destructive, they will eat wool fabric, fur, feathers and hair. Fresh air and frequent airing help to keep moths away, and if objects likely to be attacked are stored in a confined space, the old fashioned mothball will certainly help. So will a few crystals of paradichlorbenzine. Rentokil make Mothproofer which is a spray for furniture and carpets and which not only kills the moths and their grubs, but various other beetles and insects including carpet beetles and 'woolly bears'. Rentokil Mothguards are a type of mothball for putting in boxes and drawers. Various other firms make moth-proofers in aerosols which are equally effective.

Pyrethrum can be sprayed on large areas such as curtains, either by itself or with D.D.T. to clear insect infestation and protect against it.

Woodworm. The furniture beetle, known to us as wood-worm, is the fantastically destructive little horror which will eat out almost anything it can get its choppers into, from furniture to floors, books to banisters. It will enjoy papier mâché furniture and basketwork. The little round holes are in fact made by the larvae of the creatures as they eat their way to the outside world. The holes are evidence of its presence at some time, but not necessarily of its presence now. The surest evidence of the woodworm is powdery wood dust, either on the floor beneath a piece of furniture or inside drawers etc. I know of a furniture dealer who made an absolute fortune by always carrying a bag of wood powder in his pocket, and surreptitiously depositing a small heap of it beneath each object he wished to buy, and then drawing the attention of other dealers, particularly strangers, to this irrefutable evidence. Always tap a piece of furniture which you suspect and watch closely to see if any fine powder appears. The ravages of the furniture beetle can be so bad that the whole piece of wood becomes a honeycomb of dessicated sawdust and can collapse at any time. Most of us have seen or felt a chair disintegrate under a sitter when it looked perfectly sound to the casual glance.

Originally the furniture beetle only attacked old matured hardwood. At one time, worm holes were accepted as a sign of antiquity, and occasionally a piece of oak got the shot gun treatment to make it look antique. Recently the level of furniture beetle infestation has increased enormously, and the beetle may have actually mutated to a point where it actually enjoys softwood, for softwood infestation is becoming more common. Great quantities of softwoods have been brought into the country in the last few years for house building, and this may have encouraged the beetles which enjoy softwood. The longhorn furniture beetle, which is common on the Continent, certainly prefers new soft wood. The powder post beetle prefers the sap wood of ash, oak, elm and walnut.

Walnut is especially susceptible to woodworm, but mahogany and oak are less commonly attacked. Beech is attractive to woodworm, so look out for infestation in chairs made out of beech wood.

Treatments for woodworm infestation vary from a good brushing with liquid insecticide, to injecting the liquid into the worm holes with a hypodermic or a fountain pen filler. Rentokil specialise in vermifuges and put them up in injectors and aerosols. If you have large amounts of work to do, the big Injector Spray is a good tool. The liquid can also be bought in cans of various sizes.

Treatment should be repeated after a period, according to makers' instructions, and take care to wipe away excess fluid. It is always wise to test an inconspicuous part of the furniture before using insecticides to make sure that no permanent discolouration occurs. Birdseye maple and limed oak are liable to be discoloured by the liquids.

Be liberal when treating for woodworm.

If your piece of junk is so badly infested with worm that it is about to disintegrate, you have no alternative but to cut out the bad wood and replace it with new. If the piece is just to put in a show case, or stand on a shelf, then it can be filled with resin (see under *Guns and Pistols* in section on *Arms and Armour*) or soaked in paraffin wax. These substances will run into the holes, and when set will strengthen the article considerably. Araldite is useful for this job.

Because the larvae emerge in June and July, it is a good idea to give any wood which you suspect an extra treatment in May, to kill them before they can get out and infect even more woodwork.

Rentokil also make furniture creams and polishes which contain a protective vermifuge. This polish can be used regularly or occasionally, and it is a good idea to use it on the unpolished surfaces once or twice a year to protect against woodworm.

JEWELLERY

Amber. Bits of amber made into necklaces, pendants etc. often turn up in old jewel boxes and odd lots in junk shops. Clean them with soap and water. If the amber is very dirty, rub it carefully with a little French chalk on a damp cloth. Spirit solvents of any kind should never be used on amber as they will dissolve it, for it is a kind of fossilised resin. 'Renaissance' wax polish can be used for buffing and polishing to finish off (see *Polishes*). If amber has been split it can be joined with celluloid cements (see *Adhesives*) such as Durofix used very thinly, or with epoxy resin adhesive such as Araldite.

Coral. Swabs squeezed out in weak detergent should get most of the dirt off coral, but stubborn grime can be abraded off with cotton wool dipped in fine whiting or powdered pumice. Finish with a light wax polish, and use nylon thread for re-threading coral.

Jet. Shiny black Whitby jet was very popular with the late Victorians, who used it to mourn for Prince Albert. It can best be cleaned by rubbing it with new breadcrumbs. Mend broken pieces with Araldite coloured black.

KNIVES, TABLEKNIVES, POCKETKNIVES & PAPERKNIVES

Knives with silver blades must obviously be cleaned as if silver; steel bladed knives should be cleaned by abrading with emery powder to remove stains (see *Arms and Armour*).

Clean bone and ivory handles as suggested in the section on *Bone and Ivory*. Clean old knives with ivory coloured xylonite handles with Uniglan (a product for cleaning modern melamine ware).

The most common problem with knives is that the blade has come loose from the handle, probably because the knife has been washed too often in hot water which has melted the glue. Remove the knife blade entirely from the handle and clean off all the old glue or cement composition from the tang of the blade (see Fig. 30). Then pick out all the composition from the inside of the handle with a piece of wire, or even a knitting needle. When all is clean, fill the cavity with epoxy resin and push in the spike. If the cavity is much too big for the handle and if any part of the resin will show, mix whiting into the resin to match the colour of the handle, making cement composition.

Ordinary resin can be used. Fill the cavity in the knife handle with melted resin and then heat the tang red hot and push the blade home, wiping off any surplus resin. Care must be taken not to touch the handle with the red hot blade, or you may scorch it.

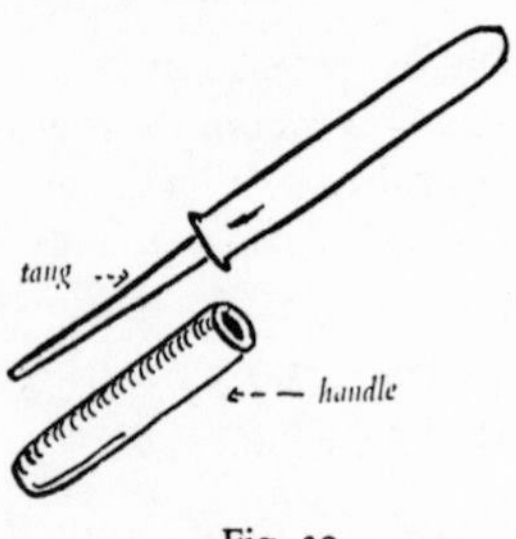

Fig. 30

LACQUER

Lacquering of polished metals. The lacquering of polished metals is suggested in several sections in this book, and various products with which this can be done are mentioned. The practice of lacquering does undoubtedly save the housewife lots of time, and for objects on permanent display, lacquering gives them considerable protection and keeps them looking nice. However, it is never a substitute for good hand polishing if the time is available, and in the long run can be an absolute nuisance. Lacquers do not last for ever, and although some can be removed quite easily with solvents others may have to be painstakingly peeled off. Junk and antique dealers hate lacquer, because they often buy objects which have been lacquered and which need re-furbishing, and as they have no means of knowing what lacquer has been used, it can be a problem to remove it, and it takes a lot of time. Therefore, if it is in your mind to sell, sooner or later, the object you intend to lacquer, think again. It might reduce its value.

Lacquers are also used to impart colour to metal objects, and in fact however colourless lacquer seems to be, it does in some subtle way alter the colour of the metal. There is really no substitute for the surface colour and sheen obtained by polishing and the surface of lacquer is so brilliant that the effect can be too bright and reflective. It is a matter of taste really, and of convenience, the long lasting finish being a blessing, especially where there is much metal which would otherwise have to be polished.

Ercaline is a general purpose lacquer to be sprayed or brushed which is suitable for all metals, particularly copper, brass and bronze. It comes in different colours: colourless, pale gold, medium gold, deep gold and copper, and it must be used with its own reducer. It gives a brilliant finish, and this will last under normal conditions for some five years or more. It can be removed with solvent when it begins to break up.

Frigilene lacquer is specially suitable for silver as it imparts no colour to the metal. It is made in various grades.

Starlac is a brush-on lacquer suitable for bronze and other metals. It comes in the same range of colours as Ercaline. It is suitable for lacquering metallic odds and ends, such as buttons, belt buckles, metal fittings and brackets.

Joylac is another brush-on lacquer which I have found useful.

Black cellulose lacquers such as Velvoid are made for lacquering brass, copper, tinplate etc. to various black finishes, bright, silk or eggshell.

Auraline is a cellulose bronze medium eg. suitable, when mixed with gold bronze powder, for reconditioning the insides of cigarette cases etc. It should be sprayed on.

Lacquer for Wood. I have classified the recently developed high glaze finishes for woodwork as 'lacquer' because their purpose is to impart high-gloss impervious and protective finishes which obviate the need for continual polishing. Their function therefore is exactly the same as metal lacquer.

There are various proprietary brands on the market, and they have endless uses. Once again I do feel that for all their excellence they do not replace the polish and finish and colour achieved by conventional methods. They do make everything look new and shiny, which is not an effect one wants on old objects.

Ronseal Hardglaze is painted on to the object across the grain of the wood and left to dry for eight hours. It can then be sanded if required and another coat put on. If Hardglaze is left to set for a week and then rubbed down with a fine abrasive such as Tripoli powder on a pad soaked with linseed oil, it can be brought to a mirror finish with a final clean with metal polish.

Ronseal also make a non-shiny preparation called Mattcoat which will seal surfaces without making them shiny. It can also be used as a filler for small blemishes.

Japanning. The Japanese developed furniture lacquering techniques to a fine art, and we are all familiar with that often hideously decorated lacquered furniture that our grandfathers so assiduously copied from the few examples of the real Japanese work. Small lacquer boxes and pieces of furniture still appear in junk shops and they can be cleaned, polished and restored to look quite attractive.

In places the decoration may have flaked off, and there may be a gesso surface underneath. Replace this by painting on fresh coats of gesso (see *Gesso*), to build up the pattern, and repaint the decoration by hand. I see no reason why modern lacquer paints should not be used to restore decorated lacquer work, although you may get problems where gilded areas are involved. The cleaning off and replacing of gilding of any kind is difficult to do well. Solvent will probably remove the gilding completely, and to re-gild, see the section on *Gilding*.

LEATHER

All kinds of leather objects abound in junk shops, and many things have leather parts to them. There are the leather grips and scabbards of swords, leather powder flasks, Victorian trinket boxes, dressing cases, leather bound books, and furniture with leather tops or upholstery.

The British Museum Leather Dressing (see recipe under *Beeswax*) is an extremely useful dressing and preservative especially good for leather-bound books. Wipe the dressing on to the leather with a soft rag, taking great care as the mixture is highly inflammable. Leave the books to dry for several days before polishing with a soft cloth or a soft brush. This dressing is also good for leather upholstery or desk tops or the leather covering of boxes, in fact for any delicate leather work.

Leather which has 'died'—begun to go rotten and powdery—will be helped by being treated with a mixture of alcohol and castor oil, 30 parts of castor oil to 20 parts of alcohol. Next day put on a dressing of pure castor oil.

Renew stitching which has gone or got weak with thread impregnated with beeswax.

If leather is very dirty it can be washed provided the job is done carefully and provided the leather stain does not run. Test with a water colour paintbrush before doing the whole job. Remember that washing may melt adhesives.

Use pure soap and not too much warm water and wipe the leather carefully. Stains on leather can sometimes be removed with white spirit or petrol, but don't rub too hard.

Proprietary fungicides will cure mould on leather.

To repair leather coverings which have come away from their base, clean off all the old glue from the under surface of the leather and the wood to which it is stuck by scraping, and re-stick with a synthetic resin adhesive (see *Adhesives*). Do this before putting on any dressings as the oils etc. in the dressings may stop the adhesives from working properly.

Painted leather objects can be treated with the British Museum dressing, but do preliminary cleaning very carefully in order not to disturb the paint.

Sheerwax and Hide Food both clean leather and feed it and are excellent for old leather of all kinds, except for suede for which they are not intended. They are simple to use and polish up very easily.

If you find something made of leather that has literally got so dry and shrunk that it will not move, or is becoming crumbly, it will sometimes respond and become supple again if liberally treated with saddle soap. Propert's saddle soap is excellent, and applications should be made on successive days until the desired condition of the leather is obtained. Wipe the soap on with a small almost dry sponge, or if it has to be worked into crevices, with a soft brush. It is readily absorbed and does nothing but good to leather.

Sometimes old leather has perished to a state where applications of leather soap cannot restore it. There is little that can be done except to replace the old leather with new. Occasionally, if leather has been painted, any blemishes can be covered with a leather dye. Meltonian Black Patent Magi-Dye will give a high polish finish.

Don't paint leather with ordinary paints, even if these have been used before.

Replacing Leather Desk and Table Tops. Hide, skiver, or morocco leather are used to top tables and this can be bought from any good arts and crafts shops. Usually the leather is bordered by a piece of veneer, and the leather is brought right up to this border and lies flush with it.

First of all the old leather is removed, and most of it will probably peel off, helped by a knife blade. The surface will then have to be made very clean and smooth, all old glue and bits of leather being taken off with glasspaper. Cut the new piece of leather with a sharp knife, bigger than the aperture to be filled, because it will shrink as it dries and it would be a pity to end up with a gap all round.

Paperhanger's paste or synthetic resin adhesives can be used to stick the leather down, but don't make the adhesive too wet, or the leather will become drenched and will shrink too much. Give the leather a good coat of glue, and give the wood surface another coat. Lay the leather carefully in place, but do not stretch it. Smooth it with a cloth pad to get all air bubbles out. When the glue is nearly dry, press the leather into the recess edge with your finger and make a mark with the edge of your thumb-nail. Then, carefully cut the leather along the edge of the veneer. Hold the knife at a slight angle so that the leather is under-cut, and the edge will be neat without raw leather showing.

Sometimes leather tops have a line of tooling round them. This is done with a special leather tooling wheel, obtainable from art shops in various patterns. Clean the wheel with a little meths to make sure no stains adhere to it, and heat it until it is quite hot, but not so hot that it scorches the leather.

Meanwhile, carefully, and without applying enough pressure to indent the leather, draw a line round the edge as a guide for the tooling wheel, or, if the line will show on the leather, make a series of dots near enough together to give you a guide. Using a ruler if you are not good enough freehand, draw the hot tooling wheel firmly along the leather. A gold border can be made by laying gold tape transfer along the edge of the tooling (see *Gilding*). The paper backing of the foil is peeled off and any surplus gold carefully brushed away with a dry water colour paintbrush. Finally the table top is given a good coat of wax dressing and rubbed with a soft cloth.

LOCKS

Most boxes, chests of drawers, cases etc. have locks, and more often than not the key has been lost. Locksmiths will make new keys for you but you may have a key that will fit. Keep all keys and try them on stubborn locks before resorting to any other method. A key may seem to fit, and yet the lock will not yield. Try to get some penetrating oil inside the lock, squirt it in with a hypodermic, or drop it in with a feather. Leave the lock for half an hour and try again.

It may sometimes be possible to get at a lock and unscrew it from the inside. Chests of drawers usually have dust pieces between the drawers. Perhaps this or the bottom of the drawer can be lifted out without damage in order to get at the lock of the drawer from above or below. Or lift the top rail above a drawer with a screw clamp or a chisel sufficiently to allow the bolt to clear, although this can so easily result in damage to the rail.

A thin punch inserted in the keyhole and hammered until you knock the lock inwards off its screws, is another rather rough way of getting the lock out, but with any luck it will only damage the interior.

The wood round the bolt can be chiselled out, but as this must obviously be done from the outside, the next step will be a repair job which may show.

Locked doors are equally difficult to open, although leverage may make enough space to get a piece of wire or a thin blade in to push back the bolt.

Generally speaking, take great care to avoid damage; it is tempting to exert that extra bit of force, and all that will result is a broken piece of still firmly locked furniture.

If I cannot open a lock by gentle means I will call in a locksmith with his assortment of skeleton keys before I start forcing things or chipping away and doing damage. A course in lockpicking is the real answer, I suppose, but I cannot tell you where to take one!

Having opened your box or whatever, if you do have a key which fits, oil the lock and work it until it acts freely. If the lock is still stubborn it is usually possible to dismantle it carefully and clean and polish each part. Jenolite rust remover, Plus Gas, or any good penetrating oil will help, and then the parts should be washed with turpentine substitute, and all rust abraded off with steel wool. A final clean and a light coat of good machine oil will finish the job and the lock can then be reassembled.

Of course locks can be collected for their own sake, and the same remarks apply. Each lock will have to be stripped—care being taken to make a drawing or notes of how it is assembled—each part cleaned with rust remover and then polished and lubricated before reassembly. It may be necessary to make new parts and this will require study of casting techniques and metal working. On the other hand, it is often possible to cannibalise locks to make repairs to a good one. The lock collector soon acquires a box of spare parts which can, by filing, be made to fit.

Old locks were sometimes very beautiful, as they were part of the decoration of the box or door that they locked, and all the decorative metalworking techniques were used—damascening, moulding, engraving, wrought iron, blue steel etc. Even the keys had 'bows' or handles which were highly decorative. A good idea, this; I think it must have been much easier to remember that the key for the treasure chest was the one with the dragon on its handle, than to have to try a whole lot of ugly ring bowed keys as one does today.

MARINE JUNK

Bits of ships and boats, used decoratively or made into other things, abound. The materials are usually brass, mahogany, and teak, and the cleaning and repair of these objects is covered in the sections on those materials. It is outside the scope of this book to describe *how* marine junk may be made into other things, but to give you some idea of what I mean, I possess a brass binnacle lamp (beside the clock in Fig. 12) made into a small electric lamp which lights an alcove; a paperweight made from a lead and brass detonator horn from an old sea-mine; and a splendid small mirror made from a mahogany and brass porthole from a trawler (see Fig. 31).

METALWORK

Gold is the most indestructible of metals because it is so resistant to tarnish and corrosion. The wonderful collection of gold jewellery in the British Museum looks as if it were made yesterday and yet it is many hundreds of years old.

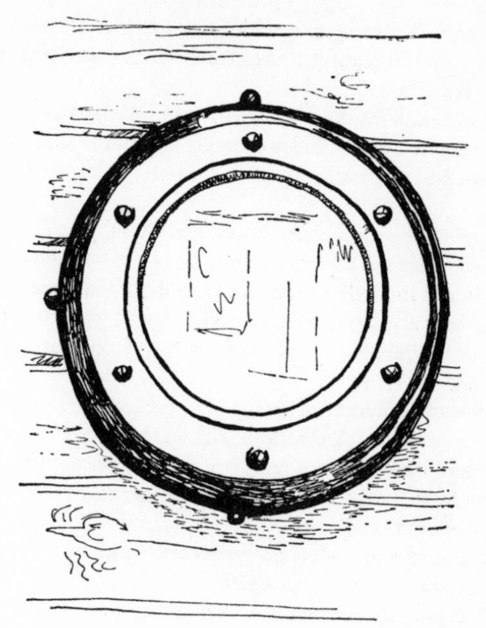

Fig. 31

Needless to say it has been carefully cleaned and restored, but its colour, its patina, its beauty are its own, inherent in the quality of the metal, as well as the beauty of the design.

I'm not suggesting that such things will come your way as junk, but nevertheless small gold articles and gold trim are everywhere, and may need cleaning. Normally a wipe with water and mild soap, or pure detergent is all that is necessary. If the gold has tarnish that will not come off, then it is not pure gold, but has other metals in it. Ammonia solution will probably clean it.

Finally a good polish with a soft cloth or chamois will bring up a beautiful shine. Remove any scratches with jeweller's rouge.

Goldsmith's polish with coarse and fine grades of crocus powder or rouge (oxides of iron), and finish with swans-down and rouge to get a perfect finish.

Copper. Copper objects acquire a bluish green coating which is not too hard to remove. Make a paste of powdered chalk and methylated spirit and rub it on with a soft cloth. The copper should then be polished with crocus powder or fine whiting and finished with a proprietary metal polish.

A weak solution of oxalic acid rubbed on to spots of corrosion with a soft cloth will loosen them. If fiercer abrasive methods are used to clean copper, they will scratch the metal, and then the scratches in turn must be polished out.

Remove water spots on copper with whiting and spirits of turpentine made into a paste.

The old fashioned method of cleaning copper was to rub it with half a lemon dipped in salt, and this is still good, as it does not affect the patina of the metal.

Thoroughly cleaned copper objects can be lacquered (see section under *Lacquer*).

Because copper was the metal most frequently used for kitchen pots and pans (visit the Royal Pavilion at Brighton some time to see the most fabulous collection), there were itinerant tinkers about who called frequently to mend copper pots and pans, and it is quite common to find copper saucepans, preserving pans etc. with handles which obviously don't fit. This doesn't mean to say that the pot isn't genuine, just that it has been incompetently mended at some time.

If it is necessary to re-rivet a handle to a copper pot (see Fig. 32), remove the old rivets by filing off the tops until the stub of the rivet can be knocked out with a punch. Clean up the holes in both pot and handle, and choose a rivet slightly longer than the hole it is to mend. Insert it from the inside, and holding the base of the rivet on a hard surface, the top of a vice for instance, hammer the rivet over.

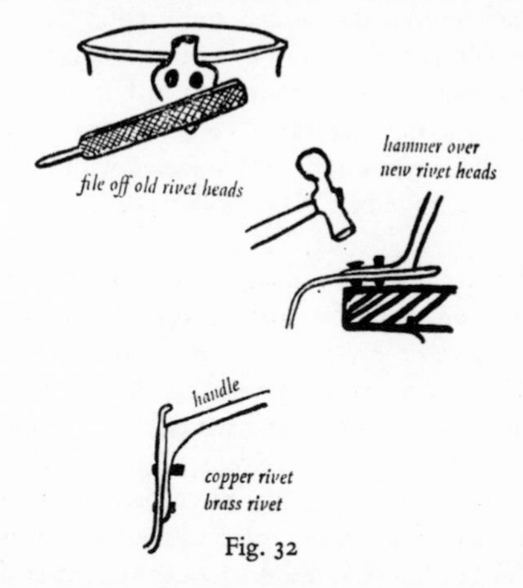

Fig. 32

If brass rivets are used, they should be only slightly longer than the rivet hole, as brass when hammered over to form the rivet head, may split round the edges, which is unsightly. Provided there is enough metal to hammer over into a small ridge, it will be sufficient to hold the rivet. When using copper or other kinds of metal rivets, a much bigger flange can be hammered out without risk of splitting.

If it is necessary to make the rivet holes waterproof—perhaps you wish to use the pan as a flower vase—put a little Araldite or Plastic Padding in the rivet hole, between the handle and the pot.

Nothing containing vinegar should be cooked in a copper pan, as the acid in the vinegar reacts with the copper.

Brass screws and copper nails were commonly used in making furniture and still are; brass screws, because they do not rust, are invaluable, and copper nails are useful for restoration purposes.

Copper can be soft soldered (see *Soldering*), provided the surfaces are thoroughly cleaned and a good flux is used. Spirits of salt and glycerine, or borax, are suitable. The join will not, of course, colour match, but this could be overcome by lacquering with a copper coloured lacquer.

Copper, like brass, can be hard soldered with spelter, but this requires a forge or a good blow pipe.

Bronze. Bronze is an alloy of copper and tin, and because it is a very good metal for making castings, there are innumerable cast bronze statuettes and statues about. Unfortunately bronze corrodes very easily, and goes green when exposed to air. The colour which bronze has achieved by patination is probably the most attractive thing about it, but you may want to get the piece back to its original state. Sometimes the patina can be flaked and scraped off (use a brass brush, not a steel one), but a ten per cent acetic acid (vinegar) solution in water will take off the harder constituents of the patination, leaving a red discolouration which is easy to remove by rubbing.

It is much more likely that you will want to restore colour or patination to bronze. Various chemical bronzing fluids can be bought, but these usually give a finish which is quite easy to spot as not genuine. Their real use is for commercial bronzing and not for the restoration of junk. Various chemical bronzing mixes can be made, and the use of these is very much a matter of experience and experimentation, trial and error and no rules of thumb can be

Fig. 33
Brass lion dog on which the shaded area has been mended with solder

given. Bronze heated and then brushed with graphite will acquire a brown patination. Or make a solution of 30 parts of basic copper acetate and 30 parts of ammonium chloride in 10 parts of water. Bring it to the boil, put the object into it, and leave it there until it is the desired shade of brown.

Bronze is soldered in the same way as brass and copper.

Brass. Brass is an alloy of copper and zinc. It is probably the most widely known and used decorative alloy.

Wash dirty brass with ammonia solution to remove grease and dirt. Then clean it with a solution of vinegar and salt—one heaped tablespoonful of salt and two table-spoonfuls of vinegar to a pint of water. Finally polish with a little sweet oil on a cloth, or a proprietary metal polish. Oxalic acid and salt will remove dirt in the same way.

Really badly corroded brass can sometimes be cleaned with washing soda—immerse the pieces in a warm, fairly strong solution and wipe or brush until the corrosion comes off. If you dare to be really drastic, boil the article for several hours in a seven per cent solution of sodium hydroxide (caustic soda). Having done this, wash the object under a running tap and brush the stained parts with a very fine wire brush. Dry thoroughly and finish with metal polish.

Remove bad spots of corrosion by abrasion with emery powder on a cloth, or fine steel wool. Work in one direction only, and polish out any scratches with whiting or jeweller's rouge.

If it is possible to do so without damage, remove very dirty pieces of brass from furniture, boxes etc. before trying to clean them. It is so difficult to clean the brass without getting some of the cleaner on to the surrounding wood.

Broken brass can be hard soldered together, using spelter (see *Soldering*). The brass has to be heated to an even red heat with either a blow pipe or a forge. Borax and water is the usual flux. Spelter is laid along the join and as the correct heat is reached it will melt and bind the broken edges together.

Brass can be soft soldered or soldered with silver solder, but the join will not match and will have to be coloured with lacquer, or with Restoration Wax (see *Gilding*).

Brass can be lacquered with Ercaline (see *Lacquer*) to avoid the necessity for perpetual cleaning.

Benares ware. Benares ware is beautifully engraved, chased and embossed Indian brass. Clean it in the normal way, and lacquer it to save work, although this seems to me to be a pity, for Indian brass has a wonderful golden colour and pays for polishing.

Brush with an old soft toothbrush with a solution of household ammonia to remove the dried deposits. Take care when using ammonia to avoid splashing the skin or eyes, and follow makers' instructions. Using the same brush, apply a liquid detergent or a strong warm solution prepared from any of the well-known detergent powders and brush the affected areas. Rinse the brush thoroughly in clean warm water and brush out the grooves and chasing with water, and finally rinse the brush free from all traces of detergent.

To prevent such deposits on chased and embossed metal, apply the Brasso with an old soft bristled toothbrush instead of a cloth. Similarly polish with a duster overwrapping the brush in order that the irregularities of the brass surface can be polished out. Finally, brush lightly with a soft paint brush.

Benares ware can be brazed if broken (see *Soldering*), but this requires heating by blow lamp and cannot be done with an ordinary soldering iron. This is quite a tricky job, as the heating of the brass can spoil the look of the surrounding metal if too fiercely done.

Lead. There are not many objects made of lead around. Clean small objects by boiling in water several times and then place them in a ten per cent solution of acetic acid. This should remove the white carbonate of lead deposit. Then put the article in a weak solution of sodium hydroxide, and rinse it several times in distilled water.

Pewter. Small pewter measures, old tankards, inkstands etc., are plentiful enough, even if, like all junk, they cost more and more. Pewter collections are very attractive, especially if displayed on oak, together with a few pieces of blue china.

There are two schools of thought about cleaning pewter.

If it has been well kept, and constantly cleaned, it probably has a nice patina which shines quietly, and which it would be a crime to spoil. However, more often pewter junk has a dull grey oxidation, which if bad can be spotted and horrible, and which at best is unattractive. Rubbing with a light abrasive powder may be enough to clean this corrosion. Use crocus powder or whiting. If only a very light rubbing is needed use either of these on an oily rag, and then wipe clean with methylated spirits.

Really bad corrosion must be taken off with hydrochloric acid, but this will remove all patina as well. Make spirits of salt into a fifty per cent solution with water, and paint it on the object. Leave it for fifteen minutes and then wash it off under a running tap and work over the pewter with abrasive powder. If the corrosion is still stubborn, try increasingly strong solutions of the acid. Take care when using acid always to wear rubber gloves, and to cover all working surfaces with old newspapers. Wipe up well behind you with clean water, and destroy the acid splashed paper. The ultimate treatment is to put the object completely into a bath of the acid, and leave it for fifteen minutes. Gentle abrasion should then bring away the scale. Test as you go along to see if the grey scale is going to come off. If the article is corroded in patches, and there are parts you do not wish to treat, cover the good areas with vaseline, which will protect them from the acid bath.

Another method of removing scale from pewter is to boil it in caustic soda. Add ¼ lb of caustic soda to one gallon of water, and boil away for three hours. There is just one danger in this process. If you allow the pewter object to touch the sides or the bottom of the saucepan it will melt, so be sure to suspend it in the saucepan in such a way that it cannot touch.

Both these methods, when you have finally rubbed off

the scale, will leave the pewter dull, and you will have to start again to get a polish on it. Give it a good rub with a Brillo pad dipped in water, and then use a fine abrasive powder, and finish off with metal polish or plate powder.

Dents can be hammered out quite easily with a ball peen hammer, which is a light hammer with rounded heads. Tap, if possible, from the inside of the object, holding a piece of wood against the outside.

Breaks in pewter can be mended easily enough using soft soldering techniques (see Fig. 34). Clean the edges to be soldered until they are bright, with a file or a bit of emery paper. Make a flux with half an ounce of glycerine and five drops of hydrochloric acid. Set the two edges firmly into position. If there is any difficulty about this, it is usually possible to shape some fairly stiff wire into clamps to hold the pieces steady and firm while you work.

Fig. 34
Handle and base join of tankard both mended with soft solder

Whatever alloy is used for solder it should have a slightly lower melting point than pewter. Ordinary soft solder is a bit bright and repairs tend to show. But it can be used where the repair will not show. Do the repairs from the inside if possible. The soldering iron must be hot and retain its heat, but be a little careful, as pewter has a fairly low melting point, and it is rather easy to melt away the very object you are trying to mend.

The automatic lighting jet of a gas cooker on a flexible lead makes a good jet for soldering pewter, as its heat is not too fierce, and I have used a butane blow lamp with the jet turned down, but great care must be taken not to melt the surrounding metal if this method of soldering is used. The joint is well fluxed, and the soldering metal is laid along the join. Use the hot soldering iron to sweat in the solder by rubbing it along the join, or use the jet gently to heat both sides of the join and the solder until fusion takes place.

A special flux and solder which is excellent for pewter can be made as follows; this takes a little time and trouble and is not worth it unless you have a considerable amount of work to do.

Special flux:

Glycerine	by volume	5 parts
Zinc chloride		5 parts
Distilled water		12 parts

Zinc chloride can be made by dropping zinc into muriatic acid until the effervescing stops.

Special solder:

Tin	by weight	2 parts
Lead		2 parts
Bismuth		1 part

Melt the metals together in a ladle. Make some grooves in a piece of wood, and pour in the molten metal, and when it cools you have a pewter solder wire (see Fig. 35).

Use a gentle flame and heat the solder above the cleaned and fluxed metal, heating the metal gently at the same time, and the solder will run into the join and fuse.

Fig. 35

Having effected the repair, file away surplus metal, and rub down with abrasives until the join matches the surrounding metal. If the repaired areas are too bright, the careful application of a little nitric acid will darken them.

To replace the broken glass in the bottom of a tankard, remove the old glass and get a glass merchant to cut a matching piece. If the old glass was held in by a flange, it may be possible to bend the flange back sufficiently to get in a new, perhaps fractionally smaller glass. Make a bed of Araldite so that the glass will set in and be watertight. Tap the pewter flange carefully back into place again and leave cement to set.

If it is not possible to bend the pewter flange, it may

have to be filed right out, and the glass set into cement and a new flange cut and cemented in. To solder in a new flange without breaking the glass is a difficult job for the amateur.

Never store pewter in oak drawers or cupboards, because oak gives off volatile acid which will corrode the metal.

Britannia metal. Pewter is an alloy of lead and tin, antimony and copper, in varying proportions. Modern pewter has a limited amount of lead in it, lead being poisonous. Britannia metal looks rather like pewter, but it is subtly different as it has no lead in it. Pieces of Britannia metal make excellent solder for pewter. Britannia metal was originally a kind of poor man's silver, for when really polished and new it could just pass for that metal. As it aged it came to look more like pewter. Then, when electroplating was invented, Britannia metal was used as a base metal for plating.

To clean and mend Britannia metal, work as for pewter.

Silver. The kind of small pieces of silver which may come into your hands will often be damaged, and to restore silverware of any kind to its original state takes some doing. The art of the silversmith takes years of learning and practice, and anything other than the most simple of repairs cannot be carried out without the necessary tools and equipment, or without risk of damage even worse than that which you are trying to repair. I would suggest that the collector who intends to concentrate on silver takes steps to learn the art, either by attending classes at local technical colleges, or by studying some of the very excellent books on this subject.

Elementary work with silver is not difficult, in fact I learnt it at school when I was about thirteen, and made some pieces of jewellery which held together for a few years.

Solder broken pieces together. First, thoroughly clean the edges to be soldered by scraping or abrading them. Then set up the two pieces for soldering, if necessary tying them into position with binding wire of a suitable gauge from 18 gauge to the finest according to the needs of the job in hand. Do not match the edges too tightly or no room will be left for the solder to penetrate and make a join, and when the object is cleaned the surface solder will just be rubbed off and the join will fall apart. Paint flux made from powdered crystals of borax moistened with water on to every part of the join. Dip small panels of silver solder (which can be bought in different grades, Hard, Medium and Easy), previously clipped from the sheet of solder, in flux and lay them along the join. Then heat the whole join with a blowpipe, and at the right temperature the solder will melt instantly and join with the silver. Be careful only to bring the part of the metal on which you are actually working to red heat. At the same time the whole of the work should be heated to some extent, or else differing rates of expansion will cause an imperfect join.

Usually when silver objects need resoldering, it is along a previously soldered join. It may be necessary to take this apart altogether, and the remaining old solder will have to be melted out. One of the problems is that the solder may have a slightly higher melting temperature than the surrounding metal, which will itself melt before the solder does, and then there will be an even larger hole to repair. When mending silver plate objects, the melting temperature of the base metal may vary even in different sections of the same object when different base metals have been used. The gauge or thickness of the base metal, as well as its type, will affect the melting temperatures, and care must therefore be taken. Even experienced silversmiths find this kind of work tricky.

When the soldering has been done, dip the work in a pickle—a mixture of hydrochloric acid and water, one part of acid to ten parts of water, or sulphuric acid in the same proportions. *Always* add acid to water, not vice versa, or you may get an eyeful of pickle. When handling silver objects in pickle, use copper tongs, as iron tongs react with the acid and cause coating on the silver.

A lot of work must now be done to clean up and polish the join and the surrounding silver. Remove any scratches and bits of solder with needle files. Then remove the file marks with 'Water of Ayr' stone dipped in water, rubbed with a circular movement. Then polish the stoned parts with fine emery sticks.

Next, using a brush, polish with a mixture of fine pumice powder and oil, followed by a polish with tripoli, then with jeweller's rouge. In other words, proceed from the coarse file to the finest rouge by stages. The requirements of the job will dictate in detail the methods of applying the abrasives and the number of different grades it may be necessary to use.

If the firestain, as it is called, which has been made on the object in the course of soldering does not come off in the polishing process—in other words, if elbow grease doesn't shift it—you can get a uniform colour over the whole by heating it and thus firestaining it uniformly before dipping it in pickle and repolishing the whole thing. This is rather drastic and would have the effect of removing any patina on an old piece of silver, which might be most undesirable. Failing all else you could have your piece silver plated, but this hardly seems to be restoring junk!

If your silver, after polishing, looks altogether too white, it can be coloured and there are various ways of doing this. Every silversmith has his own method. The fumes of sulphur will oxidise silver and exposure to the fumes is one way of achieving a deeper colour. Or the object or parts of it may be washed or painted with solutions of any of the chemical compounds of sulphur. Ammonium sulphide is frequently used and the best way is to make a hot solution, judging its strength by its colour. It should be pale yellow. Don't do the job in the kitchen or the rest of the family will leave home—the smell is terrible.

Apply the solution to the work and wash it off immediately the desired colour has been achieved. Then polish with a dry chamois leather. Don't let the chemical get on to your hands, or it will stain, and don't get it on to anything other than the actual silver you are treating. On set stones, for instance, it will leave a nasty stain.

Corrosion may have taken place over the years, especially near the sea, and is the result of the salt in the atmosphere causing silver chloride to form. The corrosion, if it is slight, can be removed by suspending a pure silver object for a few days in a solution of ammonia, or in ammonium thiosulphate (see Recipe 2 in *Cleaners*). Another solution which may work is a ten per cent solution of formic acid and this can be used where the purity of the silver is unknown. Put the solution in a glass or china container, and submerge the piece in it for some hours. Formic acid on cotton wool, used as a wipe, may remove slight corrosion. These formulae should be used with care, and preliminary tests should be made on objects of no great value.

Sometimes a piece of silver can be in such a terrible state that green corrosion covers the metal in patches. This can be removed with a five per cent solution of citric acid, but the work should only be done in tiny spots at a time, otherwise it can ruin your silver. A spot of the acid should be put on and washed off very quickly under running water. When the corrosion has disappeared, polish the article.

Tarnish can be removed by rubbing and polishing, either with jeweller's rouge, plate powder, or proprietary brands of silver polish, but obviously every time you rub you do remove a certain amount of the surface of the object, and this is to be avoided, especially on old objects or objects with any kind of inlay work. Therefore a dip is particularly useful, most of all for silver with knobs on as it does get into all parts of the work. Silver Dip, a proprietary brand, is safe and excellent, or you can make up your own dip. The method is as follows. Take a large sheet of aluminium baking foil, and line a large bowl with it. Lay on it all the pieces of silver to be treated, making sure they touch the foil. Make a hot solution of washing soda in water, about five per cent soda, and pour it over the contents of the bowl. There will be a lot of fuming and effervescing—this is an electrochemical reaction (hence the necessity for the objects to be touching the baking foil). Check frequently on the progress of the tarnish removal, and immediately an object is clear, wash it in running warm water, and polish it with a silver cloth.

French chalk moistened with methylated spirit, or water and a few drops of ammonia, will remove any stubborn individual spots.

Finally polish the object with a silver cloth; no further abrasion is needed after dip treatment.

If the object is not solid silver, but is silver plate, it is best to use Silver Dip, which is mild, and to give it just a quick in-and-out plunge before washing and drying, especially if any of the base metal is exposed.

Finally, to save cleaning your silver every few days, which can happen if you live by the sea or in a smoky city, you can of course lacquer the object with Frigilene, making sure that it has been wiped free of grease with spirit. The lacquer will last twelve months or so, but it always begins to perish sooner or later, and must be removed with an acetone solvent (see *Solvents*) and reapplied. Follow the maker's instructions when using this, or any other proprietary product. Some proprietory brands of silver polish such as Long-Term do keep silver clean for a few months at a time.

Professionally, silver surfaces are polished with coarse and fine grades of crocus powder or rouge, and finished with swansdown rouge to get a perfect finish.

Testing for metals—Silver: On some part of the object where it won't be noticed file down a spot so that if the object is plated the base metal will be reached. Then put on a spot of nitric acid solution. Standard quality silver produces a creamy grey deposit. Poor silver produces a darker deposit and base metal a green deposit. Wash and dry the spot immediately after the test has been made.

Gold. Put a spot of nitric solution on an inconspicuous part. Any alloy of less than nine carats will turn green.

Aqua regia will make gold of less than eighteen carats turn pale.

To make nitric acid solution, put a few drops of water in a glass container and add, very slowly, an equal number of drops of acid. ALWAYS add acid to water and not vice versa.

To make aqua regia, add hydrochloric acid to nitric acid in the proportion of three parts of hydrochloric to one of nitric.

Just make as much as you need of each and dispose of them by washing away down the sink after use. They don't keep anyway.

Soldering. Metal is joined by soldering. To put it simply, heated metal is stuck together by molten alloy. Various metals need different methods, different alloys, different fluxes. Soft solder, which is the silvery looking soft metal which is commonly used by plumbers, tinsmiths and others, is a mixture of tin and lead in varying proportions. It melts at a comparatively low temperature, and is therefore used to solder metals which also melt at a low temperature. Hard solder, or spelter, which can be used for hard soldering of brass and copper, is in granulated form. Silver solder, an alloy of silver and brass, can be bought in hard, medium and easy grades and can be used for soldering silver, brass, copper. Pewter can be soldered with soft solder, or with a special solder made out of pieces of Britannia metal, or made up for the job (see this section under *Pewter*).

Before any metal can be soldered it must be cleaned by filing, or rubbing with abrasives until it is bright. Flux is then applied, which prevents oxides forming under heat. If oxides form under heat the metals will not stick to one another. There are various fluxes, the most common being chloride of zinc, made by dissolving zinc in spirits of salt until hydrogen bubbles cease to form, and borax. Borax is used as a flux for silver, iron and steel; tallow is used as a flux for lead.

For soft soldering and for sweating solder into joints, soldering irons which can either be heated in a flame or plugged into the electric mains can be bought in various sizes suitable to the type of work for which they will be used. A soldering iron has a copper bit which, before use, must be 'tinned'. This is done by dipping the bit into the flux and then pressing some solder to the heated bit and allowing it to run all over it. The bit is then heated to the point where it is hot enough to melt the solder which you intend to use, but not hot enough to remove the tinning from the bit.

Once the bit has been tinned and heated, and flux applied

to the parts to be soldered, the solder is pressed to the bit and both are held just over the part to be joined; the melting solder runs into the join. At the same time the metal object which is being mended is also heated and the whole, theoretically, adheres. In other techniques, small pieces of solder are laid on the join, and the iron is used to melt them and mould or 'sweat' them into place. This can be done with the softer metals, such as pewter, but is not usually practical with hard metals.

To hard solder brass and copper, using spelter, the cleaned and fluxed pieces are set together and spelter laid along the join, the whole being heated until fusion takes place.

Hard soldering with silver solder is done by laying small pieces of silver solder along the fluxed join and by uniformly heating the whole join until fusion takes place.

The two pieces of metal to be joined are firmly held in place, and it may be necessary to make some kind of jig for the purpose, or to get an assistant to hold the two pieces together with tongs.

Filing and polishing complete the job.

Most important is the method of applying heat. For soft soldering, as described, a soldering iron may be used, but sometimes it is easier to heat the solder with a portable flame, at the same time heating the surrounding metal. Great care has to be taken with soft metals if a blow lamp is used, as too much heat will instantly burn a hole in the metal. The automatic lighting jet of a gas cooker—the type on a flexible lead—makes a very useful gentle soldering flame. Butane gas blow lamps are very good indeed, are easy and safe to light and handle and can be regulated fairly exactly. The old type blow lamp is rather a clumsy tool for the job. Forge heating is necessary for the harder metals and for wrought iron work, and there is the type of bellows blow pipe used in conjunction with a gas jet which one sees in many a traditional workshop. When hard soldering, it's necessary to get the brass and copper pretty hot, and to heat the spelter right up before it will fuse. When silver soldering, very great care must be taken not to overheat the surrounding metal before the solder has melted. When heating metal objects, the heat can be confined to some extent to the part of the object where you are working by packing modelling clay round it. This stops the heat being dissipated away through the rest of the piece.

MILDEW

Mildew is a microscopic blue, green, red or yellow fungi on objects which are damp. Mildew thrives in darkness, and will attack almost anything, leather, glue, paper etc. The best way to get rid of mildew permanently (it will usually brush or wipe off, but may return if conditions are not improved) is to fumigate it. This applies specially to papers and objects which cannot be brushed or abraded or treated with cleaners, etc. If you have an airtight box such as the one described for chloride bleaching (see *Bleaching Box*) it can also be used to fumigate books. Run a flex in through the glass tube, so that a bulb can be set up to heat a small container of thymol. Place the papers in the box, set the bulb going, put ¼ oz. of thymol in the container, and shut the box. Leave it for six or seven hours.

A solution of thymol in alcohol can be applied with a brush to various objects. A bath in a solution of potash permanganate followed by a wash in a five per cent solution of oxalic acid will also cure mildew.

There are proprietary preparations which will effectively deal with mildew and prevent its reappearance. Santobrite is a most useful preparation of this kind.

Bleach out mildew stains with Parazone or Domestos where such strong chemicals will not affect the underlying material.

MIRRORS

Mirrors can be re-silvered at home, but the results will not be nearly as perfect as a professional job. I remember the efforts made in my school, with a mixture of silver nitrate and glucose poured on to a sheet of glass. The real difficulty of this method is to persuade the solution to stick evenly, even to quite a small area.

If you do have a mirror which is not worth spending a lot of money on, but which you cannot bear to look at yourself in, the following method will make it usable. Remove the glass from the frame and rub off all the old silvering material and paint with nitric acid. Take care as with all acids. When all the traces of old silver have gone, degrease the glass by washing it well with plenty of warm water and detergent. Then rub it all over with stannous chloride and rinse it again. Dry it in a warm place and make an alkaline solution of silver nitrate in a reducing agent such as Rochelle salt (sodium potassium tartrate). If these two are slightly warmed over steam they will flow better and cover the glass more evenly. Brush or spray the liquid on very carefully and leave it until it is quite dry, then varnish it with shellac, and when that is dry and hard, brush on a protective layer of paint. If any fingerprints or the slightest grease mark have been left on the surface before applying the silver nitrate, nasty spots will appear, so the cleaning is all important.

Many old mirrors have just a few bad patches and spots close to the frame. In this case, particularly if they are quite large, resilver the bad parts, but it is advisable to clean off all the old paint and shellac first so that the surfaces to be touched up will be as clean as possible, especially where the old and the new silver nitrate edges join. The whole area of the glass can then be painted with shellac and protective paint.

If you have a really old mirror which is in bad condition, resilvering can reduce its value quite considerably, even if done by a professional, who will be reluctant to do the job, as the old glass will be very much thinner than in modern mirrors, and also have some irregularities, which makes a perfect finish hard to obtain. In this case you alone will have to judge whether you want an old mirror to look at or in.

When cleaning the surface of the mirror, care should be taken not to let moisture in round the frame as this causes those unsightly spots. Proprietary window cleaning preparations will clean off smear marks, or else a preparation of equal parts of water, methylated spirit and paraffin.

Sometimes a mirror which is in good condition can be vastly improved by re-framing it in a picture frame of suitable size and shape (see section on *Framing Pictures*).

MOULDING AND CASTING

The making of moulds and the taking of casts or pressings is an extremely useful technique for the restorer, and is described in the section on restoring china. Moulds can be used to restore old picture frames (see *Framing*) and to restore moulded work on furniture and fittings. See under *Fillers and Cements* for details of various materials useful for the final positive mould.

Moulds can be made with plasticine, dental impression compound (Paribar), liquid rubber such as Qualitex, or with plaster of Paris.

A pressed mould is made by pressing a flexible substance on to a pattern such as a piece of picture frame moulding.

The mould is carefully removed, and here it should be noted that plasticine is a suitable material where only a single positive is to be made and the moulded section is not undercut in any way. If the moulded section is undercut, it will not be possible to remove the plasticine without damaging it and a dental impression compound such as Paribar, which is warmed and made flexible before being pressed on, and then left a short while to harden, but which retains sufficient flexibility to be removed from the pattern without damage, is more suitable. Moulds can be made by pouring plaster of Paris round the pattern (see *China Repair*); this will have to be done in sections so that undercutting is avoided, or by pouring liquid rubber round the pattern, being much easier to remove from the pattern without breakage. Where the object to be moulded can be separated from the whole it is fixed to the side of a container—which can be a wooden box, or just made of thick plasticine—in such a way that no part of it except the end fixed to the side is in contact with anything, thereby allowing the plaster a free run. When a mould is to be made on a part of an object, a container of plasticine will have to be set up around it into which to pour the plaster or liquid rubber.

Having made the mould, which is a 'negative', a positive is made by filling the mould with any suitable filler, either poured or pressed. The filler having dried, the mould is removed and the positive cast is tidied up and stuck into position.

Because not all substances can be placed together without sticking, parting agents may be necessary so that mould, pattern and positive will not stick to each other. Plasticine and epoxy resins must be separated by cellulose acetate, and silica grease (Releasil 7) is frequently used as a parting agent. Note is made of the parting agents needed in the various sections, and care should always be taken to follow manufacturers' instructions in this respect.

NEEDLEWORK

Samplers, Tapestry, Embroidery, Berlin Work, etc. Before cleaning any of these items, check most carefully that the colours are fast. Put the sampler on a sheet of blotting paper, and press it gently with a piece of damp cotton wool. If no colour seeps through on to the blotting paper, it will probably be safe to wash it very carefully, but the test should be done on all the colours used, as some are more liable to run than others, particularly reds and blues. The water for washing should never be more than lukewarm, and a liquid detergent such as Stergene is safer than a powder, as it will leave no deposit. Place the sampler in the prepared solution, making sure that it is not too strong, in a dish large enough to keep the material flat all the time. Paddle the sampler gently up and down in the detergent a few times, and then rinse it two or three times in the same way, in distilled or previously boiled water. Dry it flat in a warm place.

If the sampler is not colour-fast, it will have to be dry cleaned. Many large firms are quite prepared to tackle delicate work, but first make sure that the firm can handle this specialist work before parting with a treasured sampler. If you are unwilling to send it away, dry cleaning can be tackled at home. Dip the sampler in a bath of carbon tetrachloride, or turpentine substitute. Both of these substances are unpleasant to handle in large quantities, so work in a well ventilated room.

There is only one really safe method to clean a very delicate sampler or piece of embroidery, and that is to dust it with potato flour. Slightly warm the flour and put a quarter-inch layer on to the material. Before it cools completely, brush it off with a very soft brush, such as a baby's hair brush.

When a sampler has been cleaned, it is well worth re-backing and framing it. The simplest method is to buy a ready-stretched canvas from an art shop, a little bigger than the sampler, which should be stitched on to the canvas with good quality silk thread. Keep the stitches as small as possible. For ideas and ways of framing your sampler, see the section on *Frames*. The fabric should not press against the glass, so insert a narrow mount of thick cardboard, which can be cut so that it is invisible when the job is completed. The back of the frame should be sealed as well as possible to prevent dirt seeping in again.

Tapestries can be dealt with in the same way as samplers, the only difficulty being their size. The easiest way to dry a tapestry is to place it on a sheet of polythene and use a hair dryer very carefully, neither too hot, nor too close.

Mount a tapestry which is to be hung on a wall on nylon or terylene net, by sewing it evenly and firmly. Then attach hanging hooks or rings to the nylon, not to the tapestry. This avoids a lot of strain and tension being put directly on the tapestry.

OPTICAL INSTRUMENTS

Old telescopes, sextants, binoculars, opera glasses, microscopes, cameras etc, sometimes turn up in junk shops and have to be restored. Clean all metallic, leather, mother of pearl etc, parts as described in the sections on these materials. As for the instruments themselves, great care should be taken. Lenses with blooming should not be touched by the amateur; in fact any cleaning of lenses which involves more than just a brush with a soft sable lens brush to remove dust, or a gentle polish with a special lens cleaning cloth or paper, is work for the expert.

The resilvering of optical mirrors is also an expert job, and while it may be possible to dismantle, extremely carefully, a telescope or a pair of binoculars and clean the lenses up a bit, it can be difficult to get the pieces back together again in proper order and with the prisms etc. in exactly the right position.

Display rather than use is probably your aim in restoring optical instruments, and in this case expensive expert work would not be justified. I suggest that you get hold of a good book on lenses and optical instruments before trying anything difficult.

ORMOLU

Ormolu clocks and ormolu decorated furniture are made of wood with added pieces of brass decoratively cast and sometimes gilded as well. Once ormolu was a bit of a joke and to have an ormolu clock on the mantelpiece was a sign of bad taste. Things have changed, however, and ormolu is much sought after. There is still quite a lot about and it is always turning up at sales and in junk shops.

Real ormolu, from the French 'd'or moulu' which means gold ground down to a fine powder and used in a mercury amalgam for gilding, needs very careful cleaning. Wipe gently with very weak ammonia to remove grime, and increase the strength of the solution gradually until the dirt comes off. But don't let ammonia get on to any wooden parts of the object or it will lift the varnish.

However, it is unlikely that you are going to have a piece of this real ormolu as junk. More likely what is now known as ormolu will come your way. This is a kind of brass made of equal parts of copper, zinc and tin, or sometimes just copper and zinc. Sometimes the object made of this alloy has been gilded as well. The cause of tarnishing on ormolu is that the brass sweats through the gilding.

Ammonia solution is equally good for cleaning English ormolu, and a scrub with a soft brush in soap and warm water with a little ammonia will probably be sufficient. To remove obstinate dirt on gilding, brush the surface with a solution of 2 parts alum, 65 parts nitric acid, and 250 parts water. Wash carefully and dry. This solution can be used on gilding, but it must be stressed that gilding is delicate and is easily damaged. Ormolu may have to be regilded if the gilt is damaged.

There are many modern gilt waxes and liquid leaf paints which give excellent results and are far easier to apply than gold leaf. These are described in more detail in the section on *Gilding*. It is important to choose a colour gold which will give the right effect and a product which can be applied easily to the whole part. On the whole the gilt waxes give the best finishes, but the liquid leaf is easier to apply to intricate surfaces—the wax being rubbed on with a finger—the liquid being painted on with a brush. Lastly paint with water colour varnish to preserve the liquid leaf.

Nitric acid solution can be tried on French ormolu, but only in a one and a half per cent solution, and then put on and wiped off immediately.

Failing these cleaning methods, the work must be done by an expert restorer as it involves the handling of highly poisonous chemicals.

Ormolu may have been lacquered at some time and then the old lacquer will have to be removed if it is to be cleaned properly. Acetone type solvents will usually remove old lacquer (see section on *Solvents*).

Another cleaner for ormolu can be made with:

1 oz. sodium hydroxide (caustic soda)
3 ozs. sodium potassium tartrate
1 quart distilled water.

A careful wipe with this cleaner may lift otherwise stubborn stains.

Before applying any of these cleaners over the whole area of the object, try cleaning a small spot of the ormolu on a part of the object which doesn't show, and always remove cleaners and solvents with water, and dry well before the final polishing or finishing.

After treatment ormolu can be polished with Renaissance wax or lacquered with Ercaline (see *Lacquers*).

PAPIER MÂCHÉ

Papier mâché was made by boiling old coarse paper, running off surplus water and then beating the mixture until it formed a thick paste. A little gum arabic was added to help bind the mixture, which was then pressed into moulds. Papier mâché can also be made by tearing up newspaper and soaking it for twenty-four hours. Pour off all excess water and make a flour paste and mix it with the pulp. This can be moulded, or used to fill small holes, but it will shrink a little. It can be used to repair old papier mâché objects, but will have to be sanded to fit, and secured with adhesive.

Another old form of papier mâché was made by pasting sheets of paper together to make boards which were then painted.

Various large and small articles were made of papier mâché and inlaid with mother of pearl. The mother of pearl was glued to the surface of the papier mâché in patterns, and the surface was brought up to the level of the mother of pearl by repeated layers of a special varnish. The mother of pearl was cleaned off with pumice powder when the varnish was dry to remove any stray varnish.

To repair any such papier mâché objects which come your way, you can either go to the trouble of making papier mâché and fitting it to match, or use filler made from epoxy resin and whiting or kaolin, sanded down and painted with black lacquer. Mother of pearl pieces can be copied and stuck into place. Cut mother of pearl with a fine saw or a sharp knife.

PARAFFIN WAX

Paraffin wax is white wax made by distilling petrol, and is very useful to the restorer, particularly for strengthening all kinds of damaged objects. It is useful for filling bone and ivory, gesso and worm-eaten wood, and it does strengthen things considerably but not enough to allow for them being handled much. Best really for showcase pieces or to save something that is very far gone.

Paraffin wax darkens wood.

Paraffin wax can be used as a polish for plaster casts. The cast is heated and liquid wax brushed into it. When it is dry, polish the surface with French chalk.

PERSPEX

Perspex is a clear material used to simulate and replace glass. It has the great advantage that it can be worked with woodworking tools, and can be shaped to simple forms by heating. It can be stuck together with Tensol cements (No. 6 for indoor use and Nos. 3 and 7 for outdoor use). Solvents (chloroform or ethylene dichloride) soften perspex, and the softened parts will adhere to each other, but not with great strength. Perspex can therefore be used to replace glass, but not where heat is involved (e.g. lamp glasses) over 80 deg. C.

Take care when working perspex with tools, such as power or twist drills, or when putting pressure on, to see that the perspex is properly supported on a flat surface, or it may split or star. It is neither as brittle as glass, nor as solid as wood.

Perspex comes clear, and in a hundred colours, so it is really very versatile.

PICTURES AND PRINTS

Water-colours. Water-colours are very difficult to clean, and first it is best to know what *not* to do. Don't immerse them in water, for the colours will run. Don't use a rubber or an eraser, as the colours may lift with the discolouration. Dirty marks can sometimes be removed by being rubbed with breadcrumbs, but even this must be done very carefully to avoid lifting colour. Remove grease stains with benzene, petrol, or pyridine, applied with a brush. These can be left to evaporate and dry as they will not stain the picture.

Much of the discolouration on old water-colours, prints, pastels and drawings comes from the backing. So often these pictures were mounted with glue or flour paste just slapped on over the whole back surface of the picture, and these organic materials are ideal for the growth of fungus and moulds which make fox marks, and stain from the glues and backing boards themselves discolour the picture. There isn't a lot of point in cleaning such a picture unless the source of the trouble is removed. But it is not so easy to strip a picture from its backing, as it cannot just be soaked off like an old stamp, or the colours may run. Prints can be soaked off only if there is no likelihood of paints or inks running.

The only way to shift a water-colour is to cut it away from its backing, working very carefully from the back with a very sharp scalpel or a razor blade. Having removed the backing, sterilise the back of the picture with thymol solution or Santobrite so that the fungus will be killed and won't just start growing again as soon as you look the other way. Then remount the picture as required.

Chlorine solutions can be used very carefully to bleach out stains, but the chlorine will have to be washed out with a brush, and retouching may have to be done if any colour has lifted. Fox marks, the small brown spots which so often mar old pictures, can be spotted out with a solution of equal parts of hydrogen peroxide and industrial methylated spirit. Use clean white blotting paper and a fine brush, and work very neatly, blotting as the marks begin to fade and then working again with the brush.

As a general rule water-colours are hard to clean and very liable to damage, so if you think you may have acquired something valuable, take it to an expert.

Holes. Holes in water-colours can be patched, and this takes a little practice so try it first on blank paper. Get some paper which as near as possible matches the paper on which the picture is painted. Paste it very carefully into position with weak size or starch paste (see under *Books*). When the repair is dry, work on the edges of the hole with india-rubber until they are slightly frayed and the papers will gradually blend. Turn the picture over and work on the back in the same way, continuing until the join becomes really neat. Be careful not to go too far and rub another hole right through both thicknesses. It will then be necessary to repaint the area, but paint won't take well on rubbed paper. Brush it with a very weak solution of cellulose acetate in water.

Prints. Prints will take rougher treatment than will water-colours, as no pigments are involved, only printing ink, which is waterproof and will not be hurt by bleaching. The exceptions to this are some Japanese prints, which are made with soluble ink, and which must be treated as if they were water-colours.

Prints may have to be removed from their dirty backings as described in this section under *Water-colours*, but if you check carefully on a corner of the print to make sure that the ink does not run, it can be soaked off by floating it on clean cold water until the glue is dissolved. Dry the print between sheets of clean white blotting paper before working on it further. A rather gentler method recommended for valuable prints is to make a sandwich of the print between, in this order, a thick sheet of plate glass, a sheet of white tissue paper, then the print, several sheets of clean white blotting paper thoroughly soaked with water, and lastly, at the bottom, another sheet of glass. Lay the whole thing flat on a table and put a heavy pile of books on it and go away for several hours. When the sandwich is dismantled, the print should peel away from its backing.

For full instructions for bleaching prints in chlorine gas, see under *Bleaching Box*. Fox marks can be spotted out with a solution made up as suggested under *Bleaching*, or they can be treated by immersing the whole print in a bath, either as described in *Bleaching* or in a two and a half per cent solution of Chloramine T., which is a white bleaching powder. Wet the print first in cold water (this is important in order not to get patchy effects) and then put it into a bath of the bleach. Photographers' developing trays make good baths for this work. Remove the print from the bath and rinse it in clean water, and lay it on blotting paper to dry. Repeat the treatment until the marks disappear.

Wash dirty prints in pure detergent and water, working with a large soft paint brush. Always lay the print on a sheet of glass and don't handle it more than necessary. Rinse off all the detergent when the job is done, and dry the print on blotting paper.

Iron creased prints smooth by placing them on a sheet of glass, and covering them with damp blotting paper, and then iron them carefully with a warm, not hot, iron.

When remounting use a paste made with pure starch (see *Books*) and boiling water, but add a little formalin to stop fungus growth.

Pastels. There is almost nothing that you can do to a pastel to clean it which won't remove the chalk as well. Old pastels which have been insufficiently fixed or never fixed at all, shed chalk every time they are moved. If you see coloured dust resting in the bottom of the frame, then chalk is shedding. Remove the picture delicately from the frame and spray it lightly with P.V.A. fixative, which can now be bought in an aerosol. Allow one coat to dry and put on a second coat.

Miscellaneous. Etchings, aquatints, lithographs, linocuts, woodcuts, prints washed in with water-colour, steel engravings, drawings, all kinds of pictures find their way into junk shops. There are those amusing Victorian pictures which tell a story, or blatantly moralise. As a general rule, treat all pictures with care and never immerse in water or touch with a rubber or any kind of bleach until you are quite sure there is no instability of any kind. Always test first on a corner of the picture. Clean white bread makes a useful cleaner for most surfaces, and sheets of white blotting paper are essential for cleaning, drying, and mopping up. But be careful once blotting paper has picked up a few marks, for it can easily transfer them back again to paper. The more clean sheets you have the better.

Prints from books. Old books are a useful source of prints, and there is quite an industry going in buying up old books, taking out the prints, and framing them, either singly or in sets. Look out for books containing prints in odd lots at house sales, and in dirty corners of junk shops; you may be lucky enough to spot one before a dealer gets it. If the prints need cleaning treat them as described in the section above on *Prints*. Frame them behind mats as described in the section on *Framing*. It is fun to wash in water-colour on the prints using fairly sober colours. Light pencilled bands and a stripe of pale colour enclosed by pencil bands round the print, on the white mat, tidy up the picture and give it a finished look.

Oils. Before you think about cleaning oil paintings, it is best to have a general idea of how they are made up. Pictures painted on canvas, which is in fact linen, are a series of layers. First the canvas, which is tacked and stretched round a wooden frame. The canvas is primed with a solution of glue in water, or with gesso and may also have a coat of white lead paint. The picture is painted on this primed ground with oil paints, which are coloured pigments ground in oil, usually linseed or poppy oil. The paint is further thinned with oil during the process of painting. When it is thoroughly dry, the picture is varnished.

In time the varnish discolours and gets opaque. Some varnish seems to rust and the whole picture becomes brown. It is the stripping of this old varnish, without damaging the painting underneath, which is the key process of picture restoration.

First, clean the picture with a swab of cotton wool dipped in turpentine substitute, which will remove a lot of grease and grime. If the colours then look clear and bright that may be all that is needed. A good wax polish on a pad will also clean a picture without harming it, and if left on for a while and then polished with clean cotton wool will come up well. After cleaning a picture with turpentine it may be a little dull, and need revarnishing. Use a modern synthetic varnish which will not go yellow with age. Proprietary picture cleaners will not attack the varnish and will bring the picture up well.

If, after preliminary cleaning, the picture still remains brown and dull, then the varnish will have to come off. As one of several varnishes may have been used, the trick is to find the right solvent (see *Solvents and Varnishes*). Try solvents one by one on a part of the picture which does not show; usually under the rebate of the frame.

For stubborn varnishes, a general purpose solvent made up as follows can be tried.

5 parts absolute alcohol (if you can get it)
3 parts real turpentine
1 part ethyl acetate.

Keep some pure turpentine or some castor oil on hand to inhibit the action of the solvent if it appears to be harmful. In fact, whatever solvent you are using, be sure to have the appropriate stopper at hand just in case of trouble. Remember that any solvent which will shift varnish may well shift or soften the paint underneath, and the rule is that if a solvent works too fast, and any colour begins to come away on the swab, stop work at once and swab the work with the stopper.

Start in one corner, and work gently across the picture, doing one patch at a time, and taking fresh cotton wool the moment it gets dirty. Don't take off too much varnish; try to leave a thin layer, or the picture will become very dull. In any case it will have to be revarnished. When the cleaning is done, wipe the whole picture with turpentine and leave it for a day or two to harden again. Then apply pure copaiba balsam, mixed with pure turpentine, which should bring up the colours again. Let the picture dry and varnish it with dammar varnish, picture mastic varnish or a modern synthetic varnish.

Rebacking. If the canvas backing of a picture is in poor condition, the whole thing can be relined and this is well worth doing to prevent a picture from disintegrating. The original painting must be removed very carefully from its stretcher, possibly by cutting it out with a knife. Any bending or pulling of the canvas will result in cracked paint. Use a scalpel or a razor blade. Take a new piece of picture canvas and stretch it on a wooden frame, and size it with a solution of gelatine. Put on a coat of wax adhesive.

5 parts beeswax
5 parts resin
1 part real turpentine.

Heat the ingredients gently together in a double saucepan.

When the first coat of wax adhesive has dried put on another coat. Then put a coat on the back of the old canvas, and place the old canvas carefully on to the new one, smoothing to make sure that no air bubbles are trapped. Iron the two canvases together with a heavy but lukewarm iron. Make sure that the iron nowhere touches the painted surface by using several layers of grease-proof paper, and by working on the reverse of the two canvases. When the adhesive is set, put the canvas back on to the original stretcher and you are ready to begin cleaning on a reinforced surface.

Mildew. Mildew on pictures should be rubbed off with cotton wool. Soak a sheet of thick cartridge paper in a five per cent solution of Santobrite and put it in the back of the picture. This will protect it from further fungus and mildew attacks. Best of all, hang the painting in a warm, dry room.

Sometimes old varnish gets a kind of bloom on it. This usually has something to do with the atmospheric conditions extant when the picture was varnished, and if the bloom is on the under surface of the varnish it will have to be removed. If it is on the top surface, then it can be polished off with renaissance wax polish. Bloom will appear on a picture that has been hung or stored in a damp room.

Holes. To repair holes in canvas, make a canvas patch slightly larger than the hole, and coat it well with wax adhesive (see recipe above). Put it on to the back of the picture over the hole, and carefully arrange the torn canvas as nearly as possible in its original position. Then iron the patch from the back with a warm iron, over several layers of greaseproof paper, and leave it to set. Do be careful not to blister the paint.

Retouching. The actual retouching of paintings, after cleaning and before revarnishing, or after mending holes, is possible only if you have knowledge of oil painting techniques, and some practice in them. I think that here one is getting in to very deep water for the junk restorer. It has happened before now that someone has bought a picture as junk and on cleaning it has discovered that the top layer of paint begins to come away revealing a completely different picture underneath, which has turned out to be a long-lost masterpiece. Should this happen to you, don't continue the cleaning, but let an expert have a look. You never know your luck.

Paintings on board. Paintings on board surfaces can be cleaned in the same way as paintings on canvas, but great care should be taken when handling panels, for any movement will crack or dislodge paint.

POLISHES AND CLEANERS

Recipe 1. Brass cleaner
1 heaped teaspoonful salt
2 tablespoonfuls vinegar
1 pint water.

Recipe 2. Brass cleaner
7% solution of sodium hydroxide (caustic soda).

Recipe 3. Copper cleaner
A paste of powdered chalk and methylated spirit.

Recipe 4. Copper cleaner (for water spots)
A paste of whiting and spirits of turpentine.

Recipe 5. Silver cleaner (bad tarnish)
A hot solution of 5% washing soda in water
Aluminium baking foil.

Recipe 6. Silver cleaner (extremely bad tarnish)
15% solution in water of ammonium thiosulphate, 1 part
1% detergent solution, 1 part.

Recipe 7. Silver cleaner (corrosion)
10% formic acid in water.

Recipe 8. Solution for darkening bronze
30 parts basic copper acetate
30 parts ammonium chloride
10 parts water.

Boil all ingredients together and submerge object until desired colour is obtained.

Recipe 9. General purpose polishing cloth
2 lb. shredded soap
2 pt. boiling water
4 ozs. whitening
1 tablespoonful ammonia.

Beat all the ingredients together until they become a soft jelly. Then lay some linen squares made from old drying-up cloths in this jelly and let them soak for twelve hours. Squeeze them out and leave them to dry, and use them for the final polishing of all metals.

Wood. Recipes for all home made *wax based* polishes are given under the heading of beeswax.

Other recipes for cleaners and polishes for wood are given below:

Recipe 1. 1 pt. cold drawn linseed oil
⅛ pt. spirits of turpentine (real).

The oil is strained and simmered for fifteen minutes and then allowed to cool a little before adding the turpentine. Bottle and cover tightly. It takes time to build up a good polish with this but it will resist heat from plates etc.

Recipe 2. Equal parts of:
real turpentine
cold drawn linseed oil
vinegar
granulated sugar.

Mix the liquids together and add a teaspoonful of sugar to each ½ pt. of polish. Shake well. This will clean as well as polish.

Recipe 3. As recipe two but without sugar and with ¼ part of methylated spirit.

Glass. Jeweller's rouge will polish scratched glass. Calcined magnesia and benzene mixed to a paste make a good glass cleaner.

Tortoiseshell and horn. Polish with linseed oil rubbed in with a warm hand.

RESINS AND PICTURE VARNISHES

Copaiba balsam. This is an aromatic resin got from a South American tree. It is useful in picture restoring for reviving sunken colours.

Copal. A hard resin from Indian trees. Used for years as a picture varnish, it is quite difficult to remove. Copal varnish can be bought ready made from any art shop.

Dammar resin. Made from the sap of an Australian tree. It is dissolved in turpentine to make a hard varnish which does not discolour.

Mastic. Another resin made from the sap of a tree. Mastic is dissolved in real turpentine for use as a picture varnish. It can be bought ready for use from any art shop.

Colophony or rosin. The natural resin from pine trees which is a mixture of resin and real turpentine. The turpentine is removed for use by distillation.

Shellac. This resin is obtained from an insect. It is soluble in alcohol and is bought in orange or white sheets. It is most widely used in all kinds of varnish. It can be dissolved in solutions of borax. Shellac is stored in glass or stoneware, never in metal containers.

Shellac dissolved in spirit is the basic ingredient of French polish, and the same mixture was once used frequently to varnish small objects.

Shellac should be purchased in small quantities, as it looses its properties if it is kept for too long.

SCREWS

To remove old screws may be quite difficult, and if the head of the screw gets damaged you may have to drill it out, which is always a tricky job. If the screw does not turn quite easily without undue pressure, put a little penetrating oil or paraffin round it and give it a while to soak down, then try again. Try putting the screwdriver in the slot and giving it a sharp tap with a hammer; this might loosen it. If the screw is still stuck, bring an iron poker to red heat and touch the top of the screw with it. The screw expands and when it cools again it should shrink and be loose enough to remove. Take care not to singe surrounding woodwork. A brace with a screwdriving bit will sometimes help to remove obstinate screws, provided the screw is in such a position that you can get shoulder pressure to bear on the brace. The danger with this tool is that sometimes the pressure you are exerting, and the turning movement on the brace, cause the screwdriver to jump out of its slot in the screw head and damage the wood. The screwdriving brace is an effective but not an easily controlled tool.

Hole cutting bits (see Fig. 36) can be made out of tube metal with filed teeth, the idea being that you can drill round the obstinate nail or screw and then lift it out. Even

Fig. 36

a shallow hole will, when you have removed the drill, enable you to get hold of a nail with pliers, or will perhaps free a screw sufficiently for the screwdriver. The hole will need to be pegged and re-drilled for a new screw.

When screwing objects together unless great strain is to be put upon the screw, use brass screws. They do not corrode, which is a great advantage. Brass screws are comparatively soft and easily bent, and the heads easily ruined by rough treatment. So make sure that you have drilled a suitable hole for the screw, just under size, either with a bradawl or a drill, and lubricate the screw before driving it in, with a little tallow and graphite, or even by digging it into a bar of soap. It is quite surprising how much easier it makes the job.

In the early days, screws, like nails, were custom built

for each job, and the threads were hand filed in. Sound screws of any age, shape or size should be kept, against the day when you may need them again. It is not a bad idea to drop all old screws into a jam jar full of penetrating oil or rust remover. Leave them there for a while, remove and rub dry in a piece of oily cloth before putting them in an airtight jar or tin for storage.

SOLVENTS

Various solvents are commonly used for the cleaning of wood and metal. What actually happens is that the solvent mixes with the substance you are trying to remove and makes it possible to wipe or rinse both away together. To explain what happens in simple terms, spirit varnish is a good example. Spirit varnish is made by dissolving lumps of resin in a spirit so that it can be painted on to a surface. Then the spirit evaporates, leaving an even film of the resin behind. Obviously to get the resin or varnish off, it has got to be diluted with spirit once again and turned back into something like the mixture which was put on, possibly a bit thinner, so that it can be wiped off again.

If you have layers of varnish and oil paint together, the problem is to use solvents which move the one and not the other. So that it is of the first importance to make sure what it is you are trying to shift, and then to use the appropriate solvent.

Solvents can be bought under various brand names for specified jobs, from cleaning cloths to stripping rust and paint. Into this category come, Dabitoff, Thawpit, Jenolite, Plus Gas, Movol, Solvex, Nitromors and Sprayclean etc. Dissolvex is excellent for releasing joins made with Araldite, and will tackle some other stubborn glues, especially in glass repairs.

Acetone. Acetone is a highly inflammable colourless liquid which should never be used anywhere near an open flame of any kind. It is a solvent for varnish and waxes and can be used to remove these substances when other methods have failed. It works fast and can be a bit unpredictable, and if mixed with turpentine substitute will be slowed down a little. If you are using acetone and wish to stop its action, apply kerosene. Certainly it needs handling with extreme care.

Alcohol. Alcohol is a solvent and is used in the preparation of lacquers and varnish. Methylated spirits can be used in some instances, but Isopropyl alcohol is a cheap substitute. Ethyl alcohol, which is completely free from impurities, is subject to duty, and is therefore expensive and hard to get. One way of drying fragile articles is to dip them in alcohol which will remove the moisture, and then evaporate away.

White spirit is commercial wood alcohol.

Alcohol is used in picture cleaning, but as it dissolves oils, great care must be taken.

When using alcohol, keep some turpentine or castor oil handy, as an application of either will stop the action of alcohol.

Alcohol is also mixed with other solvents.

Amyl acetate. Amyl acetate is a clear liquid which smells like pear drops. It dissolves celluloid rapidly so is ideal for removing cellulose based paints, which are in fact quite difficult to shift with anything else. It can be used on moss fabrics and colours, but not on plastics or synthetics. It is highly inflammable and should be used in a room with the windows open for you shouldn't breathe in the fumes.

You may find that repairs in porcelain have been over-painted with cellulose paints, allowed to spread across the porcelain to disguise the repair. Amyl acetate will remove this.

Benzene. Benzene is a volatile spirit which is a solvent for fats and oils, resins, phosphorus, sulphur and iodine. It is used for cleaning fabrics, and is highly inflammable. Under the name of Benzol the same solvent with added Toluene is used for the same purposes.

Beeswax dissolved in benzene (see *Beeswax*) makes a preservative coating for wickerwork.

Benzene can be mixed with other solvents, such as alcohol or with carbon tetrachloride, to get rid of stubborn staining.

Recipe 9 parts carbon tetrachloride
1 part benzene
1 part Lissapol N. (detergent).

Mix the first two ingredients, and then add Lissapol N. to form an emulsion. Use this for cleaning really dirty granite or basalt (see section on *Stone*).

Benzine or Petroleum Ether. Benzine is rather like petrol but has a lower flash point. It is used in the same way as benzene to shift grease spots in fabric. It is also a solvent for waxes and fresh resins used in varnish.

Carbon Bisulphide. Carbon bisulphide is a volatile colourless and highly inflammable liquid which gives off inflammable gas and smells horrible. It is a first class woodworm killer, and it dissolves fats, rubber, phosphorous, sulphur and iodine.

Carbon Tetrachloride. This most useful of solvents has the great advantage of not being inflammable. In fact it will put out petrol fires and is often used in fire extinguishers. It smells a bit like chloroform. It is an excellent solvent for grease and oils. Don't use it while smoking. The fumes change into a poisonous gas if breathed through a cigarette or a pipe. In fact you should avoid inhaling the fumes, and if working with it for any length of time, be sure to keep the windows open. Many proprietary brands of spot remover are based on carbon tetrachloride.

Chloroform. Chloroform is not inflammable but for obvious reasons shouldn't be used except in well ventilated conditions. It is a good solvent for beeswax, and will also remove paint stains.

Ether. Ether is an extremely powerful solvent for paints and varnishes, but it is inflammable and explosive and is best left alone by the amateur.

Ethyl Acetate. This is another inflammable solvent similar to amyl acetate.

Petrol. Petrol is too easily available and it is often used as a solvent when other safer solvents would be best. Never use it anywhere near a naked flame. A concentration of the vapour will ignite from the spark caused when throwing a light or power switch, and if petrol is in a container it may well explode if ignited. If you use it to clean silk, the friction caused by rubbing may make a spark and set the petrol off. It is a good solvent for fats, oils, bitumen, and mineral pitch.

Turpentine. Turpentine is an oil obtained by distilling the sap of the pine tree. It is a very useful oil as it dissolves resins and waxes, and various other substances. It is a common ingredient of polishes and cleaners. Because it is a solvent, care should be taken when using it for cleaning, as it may make underlying paint soft and unstable.

To test turpentine for quality, drop a little on some clean blotting paper. If it evaporates without leaving a ring, it is good quality.

Turpentine should be stored in the dark as it tends to thicken and darken when exposed to sunlight.

Turpentine substitute or white spirit. This is commonly sold for turpentine, but while it is useful as a solvent and cleaner it is *not* suitable for making high grade polishes etc.

Venice Turpentine. Venice turpentine is distilled specifically from larch and is very thick. It is used to some extent by restorers and artists.

Pyridine. This is a useful solvent for grease and oil stains, and old varnish on pictures. The refined grade should be used. It is inflammable and poisonous in concentration.

STONE

First of all the objects made of various kinds of stone, which stay in gardens: statues, bird-baths, sundials etc. These things usually get stained and dirty, which in fact improves them. There is nothing so horrible as new stone garden furniture. Limestone and sandstone form a kind of patina or crust over the years, and if you remove this, the stone underneath may be very soft and crumbly. If you must clean a stone object, try using a hose with a powerful jet and wire brush, but don't be too rough. Bad mildew stains on stone can sometimes be removed by the paper pulp method. Make a pulp out of some cheap white paper (*not* newspaper because of the printing ink). Tear the paper up small and heat it in some distilled water. Keep stirring (borrow the kitchen beater) until you have a thick pulp. This pulp is then laid three-quarters of an inch thick over the stain and left until all the water has dried out. The water from the pulp should go down into the stonework. Then as the paper dries out, it draws the moisture back to itself plus the dirt. Oil stains can be removed in the same way, except that you dry out the paper pulp first, and then re-soak it with turpentine substitute. Then proceed as before. The principle is exactly the same except that obviously when removing oil it is necessary to use a moistening factor that is solvent for oil, and will carry it out of the stone.

These are treatments for porous stones, but other stone objects, made of granite, basalt etc., can be handled a little more roughly. Encrusted dirt can be removed with water and detergent and a wire brush, or see section *Solvents* under *Benzene* for recipe, when this method fails.

Mend broken stone ware of all these types with Araldite. Araldite or other epoxy resin will mix with stone powder and colouring to match, to build up missing pieces. When using adhesive, take care to degrease the surfaces to be joined, either with detergent or with solvent, then to abrade, and then to degrease again.

Soapstone. Statuettes carved out of soapstone are quite common. Soapstone is very soft indeed and therefore must be treated gently. It can be washed with soap and water, or water and detergent, and this should remove dirt and grease. However, such treatment may leave the surface a little dull. Dry the object well with a soft cloth and give a light coat of silicone polish, or renaissance wax, and rub it lightly. A rub with a warm hand will help to get a nice finish as the warmth of the hand softens the polish a little, warms the stone, and so hastens absorption into the surface.

Sometimes soapstone figures have painted detail on them, so take care not to rub this off with soap and water, detergent, or polish. As always the problem is to clean without removing patina.

Alabaster. Alabaster statuettes, ashtrays etc., turn up in junk shops, usually broken or badly repaired with ordinary glue. Alabaster is a soft substance and doesn't like water as it is porous and water soaks into it. The acids dissolved in the water attack the stone; so *don't* clean alabaster with water. Give it a gentle wipe with a little white spirit, petrol or benzine, or paint solvent, applied with a soft rag or a soft brush. Having removed the greasy grime, clean up finally with white spirit.

If your piece of alabaster has an unsightly glue line where it has been mended, soften the glue by applying little poultices of cotton wool soaked in hot water and squeezed out, and take the join apart again. Hot water will take off the glue, and its corrosive effect is not so dangerous here as you are not working on the surface of the object where it will show. However, it is best to keep the clean alabaster as dry as possible. Warm water with about twenty per cent ammonia will remove any stubborn animal glue. Milton will bleach out really bad stains. When the bleaching is done, let the treated area dry out before attempting to polish it. It should look a little lighter than the surrounding untreated alabaster, and will then darken again as it is repolished. Having cleaned off the old glue and any staining, the alabaster can be rejoined with Durofix. Where the alabaster is chipped, it can be built up in layers with a mixture of Durofix and refined whiting.

Whiting makes the transparent Durofix look like the translucent alabaster and with a little care you should get a pretty good finish.

Having mended the alabaster, give the whole thing a good polish with a little beeswax dissolved in turpentine, or a wax furniture polish used sparingly.

Marble. You may find small marble statuettes, or marble clock cases, but the most likely marble to turn up as junk is the remains of old wash-stands. These slabs of marble have a lot of uses, not only as larder shelves, but as ornamental shelves, table tops, wall panels etc. Marble will take a wonderful polish, but it is not stain resistant, and even if it has been well skinned with polish, anything spilt on it should immediately be wiped off.

To clean marble, various methods can be used according to the age, type and depth of the stain, but any cleaning will remove the patina which old marble acquires over the years.

For general light cleaning, use good quality soap and water, with half a teacupful of ammonia added to a bucket full of clean water. (Be sure the bucket is clean.) Always use white cloths or swabs and not coloured ones when working on marble. A five per cent solution of oxalic acid will remove some stains. A paste made from powdered kaolin and benzine, laid on the stain and then wiped off, will remove oil stains. Chloroform will remove beeswax. Don't use strong acids on marble as they may dissolve it. Always remember that marble stains very easily. Marble may be stained by fungoid growth, especially if it has been stored damp. Chloramine T in a two per cent solution may shift this type of stain. Bleach out fungoid stains with very dilute hydrogen peroxide with a drop of ammonia added.

If marble has got green stains on it caused by algae, as can happen to pieces left outside, wash it with a five per cent solution of Santobrite.

Having cleaned the marble, polish it with chalk and water, but never use harsh abrasives.

Ordinary silicone furniture polish very lightly applied, or a silicone impregnated duster, will give the marble a nice finish and protect it to some extent.

Marble can be lacquered if it is to be kept indoors. A suitable lacquer can be made by mixing white shellac and methylated spirit, but an acrylic resin will do just as well. (See under *Fillers and Cements.*)

To make a good protective coat for a piece of marble which is going to stay out of doors, melt some white beeswax in white spirit until the mixture is the consistency of butter. Warm the marble in front of the fire so that it will absorb the beeswax into its surface. Wipe the wax mixture on to the marble evenly, with a soft white cloth, and remove all the surplus, so that there is no waxy surface to collect dust and dirt.

Flat slabs of marble, having been de-stained, may be given a last clean with warm soapy water, thoroughly dried and then given a good coat of silicone furniture polish. A thorough buffing with a lambswool bonnet on a power drill, and perhaps a second or third coat of silicone if necessary, and further buffing, will bring the surface up to a mirror finish which should last for years, provided it is dusted occasionally.

Marble which has chips, holes, cracks, etc. in it can be infilled with Araldite. Mix whiting and such colouring as is necessary with Araldite to get a perfect match. Araldite can also be used to join broken pieces, but the surface to be joined must be thoroughly degreased. Solvent on a fairly stiff brush should do this job satisfactorily. Abrade the surface with a stiff wire brush, degrease again, and then make the Araldite join immediately. If marble which has previously been mended with unsuitable glues is stained, remove as much as possible of the stain before making the mend, and of course all old glue must be got rid of. As with Alabaster, hot swabs will remove ordinary glue, but be careful not to use too much water.

For any large scale cutting or polishing jobs, I suggest you contact your local monument mason, as the work is a bit too difficult to do at home.

Slabs of marble can be smoothed with fine sanding discs on a power drill, and any rough or chipped corners can be tidied up in this way just as if they were wood. It is a bit hard on discs—they won't retain their cutting power for too long, but working with finer and finer discs, you can get a better and better finish. Finally polish with silicone as above. Just a word of warning, too much pressure or too fierce a disc may cause frictional heat and consequent staining, so work with a light touch.

STUFFED BIRDS AND ANIMALS

Stuffed birds and animals consist of the skin of the animal, complete with feathers or fur or hair, the skull, leg and wing bones. All else is artificial. Usually a wire frame is made which passes up through neck and skull, and down through limbs or wing bones, around which the creature is built up by stuffing with peat, or some other light and fairly inert substance. The legs and neck of birds are filled out by being wound with jute tow. Hard and fast rules for refurbishing these objects are difficult to lay down. A good clean would seem to be essential; and the creature itself should be treated with Fuller's Earth and brushed well, but carefully, in order not to pull fur or feathers. Stuffed creatures are usually mounted in cases with some kind of painted backgrounds and modelled foregrounds. A great deal can be done to brighten these up with fresh paint, and any remodelling can be done with Isopon, or with a similar material, which can then be painted. Polymer paints such as Cryla are very suitable as they are bright and opaque and can be used to do relief work.

Before setting up the case again, spray well with insecticide and mothproofer, as various insects, such as silver fish, can find their way into a case. Clean the glass carefully, and do any re-puttying carefully, as it is necessary to get a good seal on the case to keep out damp and dust. Broken glass can easily be replaced, and if the case is broken, make new sides with plywood, or hardboard painted to match.

Fox Masks. Fox masks abound in this ferocious land, and you might acquire one by inheritance, especially if you live in the country. A good brushing should keep Charles James clean, and his teeth could be given a wipe with a little domestic bleach or hydrogen peroxide if they have become yellowed. Broken teeth can be replaced by remoulding new ones in Isopon, Bondapaste, or Araldite, having taken a plasticine mould from another tooth, as described in the section on mending china. The pink mouth and tongue, if they do not come clean with a good wipe, can be repainted with artists oil paint or polymer colours, and varnished with a spray varnish or picture mastic varnish, or polymer varnish. Mothproofing is always advisable.

Other hunting trophies can be cleaned according to the materials of which they are made, hair, leather etc.

TORTOISESHELL AND HORN

Clean objects made of these things with water and soap or mild detergent, but don't use too much water, just wipe with soft swabs. When cleaned and dried, horn and tortoiseshell can be polished by buffing on a polishing wheel charged with whiting, or if this is a bit too drastic for the object, then wipe it over with renaissance wax and polish it with a soft cloth.

Tortoiseshell can be polished with tripoli or rottenstone (carborundum products) or with silica preparations such as modern metal polishes.

A little linseed oil rubbed in with the palm of the hand improves the look of horn objects such as antlers.

If tortoiseshell or horn is broken, mend it with Durofix or Araldite.

TUNBRIDGE WARE

You may come across small boxes or objects decorated with a kind of wood mosaic. Cribbage boards, tea caddies, cork boxes, all kinds of things were decorated in this way and are most attractive. The mosaic is made by glueing together extremely thin rectangular strips of different coloured woods in predesigned patterns until a block is made about eighteen inches deep. The block of wood is then thinly sliced like a loaf of bread and you have a whole lot of identical pieces of mosaic veneer which are then used to decorate the objects. It used to be possible to get assembly charts, rather like those for tapestry work. Each square of the chart was lettered, the letter denoting the wood to be used, and all kinds of patterns and pictures, squares and diamonds, landscapes, flowers, animals, local pictures etc. were made. About 160 different woods were used and a list of some of these is of interest:

Sycamore, yew, pear, boiled holly, palmyra, tulip, maple, pollard, willow, fustic, birdseye maple, cherry, English ash, amboyna, blackthorn, lime, horse chestnut, mahogany, green oak, bog oak, cocos, ebony, nutmeg, laburnum, mulberry, broom, red ebony, plane, snakewood, purple heart furze, cedar, acacia, orange, Indian rosewood, satinwood, birch, box, holly, plum, Spanish chestnut.

The industry centred around Tunbridge Wells, hence the name of the ware.

Clean Tunbridge Ware very carefully in order not to disturb the small mosaic pieces, or to dissolve the glue holding them together. First, remove the old varnish by scraping it very carefully. Spirit remover may be too drastic. Use an old knife and as it is old varnish, it will come off quite easily. If you do use a varnish remover, wipe the Ware clean with methylated spirit immediately. Then rub down with the finest sandpaper, and polish with a beeswax polish or a little Mansion polish and beeswax mixed. To give the wood a more permanent glazed finish, Furniglass can be brushed on. Brush the Furniglass on the piece in one direction only and leave it on for a few hours. If a second coat is required, lay it on the opposite direction. This can be done two or three times until you have a really brilliant finish. The last coat can be put on with a pad, and when dry, the whole should be polished with a clean soft cloth.

To repair Tunbridge Ware, use coloured plastic wood to fill in small gaps in the pattern. If pieces of veneer have been broken off they can be reglued into position with Evo-Stik 528 or Scotch Glue, but it is impossible for an amateur to make a block of mosaic and repeat the pattern, and replace it himself. There are no craftsmen left doing this work (the last, in Rye, finished in 1939), so there is no possibility of getting exact repairs done in this way. Part of a useless old piece of Tunbridge Ware will patch a good piece if the patterns are similar. Furniglass can also be used to fill in small gaps, by dropping it in.

A similar kind of Tunbridge Ware was made by putting larger square pieces of wood together to form cube patterns when cut. As these pattern pieces are considerably bigger, it might be possible to replace missing pieces by finding bits of wood in a matching colour and working them to fit.

UPHOLSTERY

The renewing of old upholstery is a skill in itself, and there are many good books on this subject alone. Chairs and sofas etc. with broken springs, torn webbing and worn material will have to be tackled by the junk restorer, and it isn't really a difficult job. Broadly speaking, one begins at the underneath and removes the material, webbing, springs, stuffing etc. in the order you come to them. When removing tacks, be extremely careful not to break away chips of wood with the tacks, and always, therefore, to work along and not across the grain. You can use a mallet and a special ring chisel, which slides under the tack heads and lifts them easily. To bash away with a hammer and an old screwdriver may be all right, but be careful. Use new webbing, because webbing which is removed is not long enough to allow for straining, although it may be good enough to be reused on shorter sections, in arms etc. A special tool for straining webbing tight is simply made (see Fig. 37). Pass the webbing through the slot and back in a loop and put the piece of dowel through the loop. The webbing is

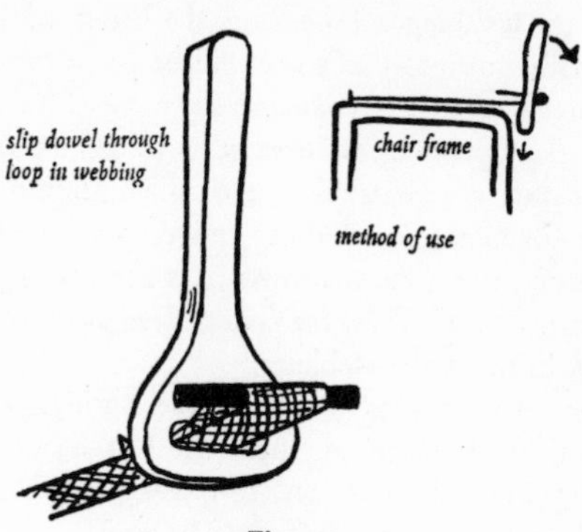

Fig. 37

then levered tight by putting the base of the tool against the frame of the chair and straining back and down. When webbing is carried round the edge of a chair or seat, make sure the edge has been rounded off. If it is sharp, it will rub away at the webbing and tear it in time.

Replace damaged upholstery springs and sew them to the webbing. Upholsterer's needles in various shapes and sizes are essential if you intend to do much upholstery work.

Stuffing may have to be renewed if it is really dirty. Clean it by taking it into the garden and giving it a good shake or a good beat. In some cases stuffing and springs can be replaced by modern foam rubber, Latex, etc. and rubber resilient webbing. Rubber webbing—not the old but extremely long wearing and efficient English Webbing, made of pure flax—is frequently used in modern furniture, and can be used as replacement in old furniture. The tension to which this rubber webbing is stretched will obviously affect the springiness of the seat. This webbing is applied at a tension of from five to ten per cent. For instance, if the chair measures 20″ from the two points at which the webbing will be fixed, the length of the webbing actually put into that space will be 19″ for a soft seat or 18″ for a firm one, stretched to fit.

When flax webbing is fitted it is folded at the ends before tacking, so an extra allowance of length must always be made for this fold. Rubber resilient webbing is not folded under, so no extra allowance is necessary, just half an inch each end to allow for fixing. Use plenty of wide-headed tacks to fix the webbing.

By the way, having removed the springs and upholstery from a chair or sofa, check the woodwork thoroughly to see if there is any re-glueing or other repairs needed. It may be your only chance to do it.

Keep all old pieces of cloth or covering that you take off to use as patterns. Even if they are in very bad condition, they will give a pretty good approximation of the shape and size.

Examine the stripped-down furniture for signs of worm and treat accordingly, and clean dust away very thoroughly with a stiff brush. As a last brushing, even if no worm is present, it isn't a bad idea to brush well with a proprietory anti-woodworm preparation, just in case. If springs have got rusty, they can be cleaned with rust remover before being replaced, or if still *in situ*, a good wipe with a rag with some oil on it, will clean things up; but don't leave surplus oil to work its way through upholstery and cause staining.

Treat leather chair covers, seats etc. with leather dressings to keep them clean and supple (see section on *Leather*). When leather covers have gone beyond repair, and the cost of replacement would be prohibitive, it is usually possible to cover with other materials. Modern synthetic imitation leather upholstery materials are excellent, but are by no means cheap.

WAX OBJECTS

Wax flowers or wax figures are usually kept under large glass bell jars, as they attract a great deal of dirt and dust. It is possible to clean them if they are in a really bad state, but it is rather drastic. The dirt should be rubbed off, by sprinkling powdered pumice on to the wax piece, and then brushing it off very carefully with a soft brush. This treatment will probably remove most of the paint as well, so that the wax will finally have to be re-painted with artists oil paints.

Clean unpainted wax objects with a little softened butter.

WOOD

It seems a little superfluous to state that wood comes from the hard part of a tree that sticks up out of the ground, but you may not know that the centre of the tree is the heartwood, and the part which grows on the outside nearest the bark is the sapwood. The colour of these two woods in a single tree can vary a great deal, and on the whole the nearer to the centre, the darker the timber. The grain is made by the lengthwise fibres, and wood is cut either along the grain or else across it. For veneers the timber is cut from small flitches, very thinly sliced so that different figuring is obtainable. Burrs are caused by outside wart-like growths on the trunk, and are mostly found in walnut, cherry, ash and amboyna, making delightful patterns from the closely formed knots. Butts are cut across the stump of a tree, and the figuring is caused by the growth of the roots. Curls or feathers are formed by the junctions of large branches, and like the butts, give a pleasant spotted appearance. Roes are caused by grain fibres twisting round a tree, and make dark flecks.

One of the problems of buying wood to-day is that often it has not been seasoned long enough to dry the sap out of it. Most wood is kiln dried anyway, which can cause uneven drying and warping; therefore any wood which is to be used for repairing old furniture should be kept under cover and in a fairly warm place for as long as possible. I am often tempted to take the odd pieces that collect, and throw them on the bonfire, but unless they are actually rotten or are riddled with woodworm, this is silly, as it is far better to mend an old chair with a matching piece of old wood. New wood will shrink as it dries out, and pull the chair out of true or weaken the mend so that all your hard work will have been in vain.

There is no real short cut to seasoning wood, and putting it in a really warm place will only make it warp, so the best thing is to work up a stock of varying woods and be prepared to keep it for a good many years.

Woods Used For Furniture Veneers And Marquetry

ACACIA (or Australian Blackwood): Light crimson in colour, and used for cabinet work and furniture. The French variety is a rich brown with a solid dark grain.

ALDER: Pale brown wood used mainly for plywood.

AMARANTH: South American wood, bright purple, but goes warm brown on exposure to air. It was sometimes used for making furniture.

AMBOYNA: Reddish to golden brown. An imported wood used for veneers and inlays in the last half of the 18th century.

ASH: White to pinkish brown, with a coarse grain. English hardwood. Used where elasticity and toughness are needed, eg. tool handles.

BEECH: A pinkish yellow wood. It is often used for small pieces, and has always been a favourite wood of the country furniture maker. It grows all over Britain and is a strong, close-grained wood which takes stain readily, and can be left natural and just polished. Furniture makers used to make furniture from beechwood and call it rosewood. Beech is more liable to worm infestation than true rosewood.

BIRCH: Yellow birch from North America is a popular decorative wood and can also be used stained to imitate mahogany or cherrywood. Imported birch is used a great deal for plywood.

BOXWOOD: Pale yellow, hard, fine grained and very even textured. Used a lot for making modelling tools. Used for inlay work in Tunbridge Ware.

CEDAR: Light reddish softwood, very resistant to insect infestations and rot, and is therefore commonly used for box and drawer linings.

HORSE CHESTNUT: Usually white, this wood is soft and light and of no great value, but Japanese horse chestnut is golden brown, and figured pieces are used for decorative work.

SPANISH CHESTNUT: Looks like oak without the silvery grain. Can be used as a substitute for oak.

EBONY: Dark and compact timber, the heartwood is sometimes totally black. Used a lot for ornamental work, but it is very hard to work and tends to crack if subjected to temperature changes. This accounts for the fact that other woods are stained black to simulate ebony.

ELM: There are many varieties of elm, yielding different coloured woods, from light buff-coloured to reddish-brown to green. The grain is coarse and forms curving patterns. It is very tough and strong and was much used for house timber and for boatbuilding and wagon wheels. However, it does warp and twist. The burr wood is excellent for marquetry.

FRUITWOODS: The wood of fruit trees—apple, pear, cherry, plum etc. is used for small pieces of inlay as the wood sizes obtainable are never very large. Pear wood is used, stained to imitate ebony.

HAREWOOD: So-called harewood is a chemically treated sycamore, brownish grey in colour. It was used for inlays in the 19th century.

HOLLY: Hard, fine-textured white wood; dyed and used as a substitute for ebony, and boiled, was used in Tunbridge Ware.

HORNBEAM: Whitish in colour, hard, heavy and tough. Used as a substitute for ebony.

KINGWOOD: Striped violet, black, and dark brown with lighter wood between, this is a rare Brazilian wood used for inlay and veneers.

LABURNUM: Yellow wood with brown streaks used for inlay and Tunbridge Ware.

LARCH: Strong, durable softwood.

LIME: Pale-coloured, soft, even-textured wood, used by woodcarvers, particularly by Grinling Gibbons who did his famous fireplaces in lime.

MAHOGANY: There are many variations of this wood, which is a close-grained, reddish-brown hardwood. Just about the most common wood used in furniture making once it had been introduced into this country in the late eighteenth century, where it completely supplanted oak for making elegant furniture.

MAPLE (SYCAMORE): In Britain the most common species is sycamore, which is hard white timber used for furniture and cabinet making. It is often used to imitate mahogany or harewood and it takes stain very well.

OAK: Light coloured hardwood with a silvery grain, which has always been used for furniture making in this country. It can be seasoned in many ways to produce woods of different colours. Bog oak is cut from trees sunk into marshy ground for some years before sawing. The resultant timber, long soaked in acid water, is hard and dark.

OLIVE WOOD: Close-grained, greenish wood used for inlays.

PINE (SCOTS): Common softwood of red or brown colour known as deal.

PLANE OF LACEWOOD: Beautifully figured wood used mostly in decorative work. It is straw-coloured with yellow flecks when cut as veneer. The yellow flecks give it the name of lacewood.

POPLAR: Whitish yellow wood sometimes with a green tinge. It is soft, light, and has an even texture, with a dull look about it.

It is difficult to splinter and is fire resistant.

ROSEWOOD: Orange streaked with dark grain, with a hard open grain. It is a South American wood used for veneers.

SANDALWOOD: Pale yellow wood used for turnery and small ornamental objects.

SATINWOOD: Lemon-coloured with a beautiful mottle, Oriental wood used for veneers and Tunbridge Ware.

SNAKEWOOD: Dark, chestnut-coloured with dark brown mottle. It comes from Trinidad and was used for veneer and inlay during the last century.

SPRUCE: Common white deal. Softwood.

TEAK: Olive brown, it comes from the Far East. It is

a naturally greasy wood and combines strength and durability with ease of working and good appearance.

TULIPWOOD: Light rose to pinkish with darker streaks of pink and red. Hardwood with soft-looking, even-textured straight grain. North American wood used for veneers, inlay and Tunbridge Ware.

WALNUT: The green rind of the nuts, as anyone who has ever picked walnuts knows, yields a dark brown stain. Walnut wood has a close even grain and it is soft to work. It takes a marvellous polish and is lightish brown with brown to black markings. Burr walnut veneer is made by slicing wood across the large burrs or warty growths on the trees. So-called oyster veneer is made by slicing across small branches.

YEW: A rich brown colour, used in inlays. Once used for making longbows.

Woodcarving

Broken woodcarving is best mended by carving a new piece to replace the broken part. This is not so difficult as it sounds, for if you are reading this book you are probably a person who likes to use your hands and can make a good try at anything practical. The biggest difficulty is to find matching pieces of wood, although with careful staining and treating a pretty good match can be made. The broken part should be cut back to a smooth surface and a block of wood cut and fitted into the space. You can then work in two ways. Either you can stick and dowel the new piece firmly into place and carve it *in situ*, or you can carve the piece separately and stick it into place. It rather depends on the type of carving to be mended. If the carving is repetitive there is no reason why you should not take a pressed mould with plasticine or Paribar as described in the *China Mending*, *Moulding* and *Framing* sections, and make a new piece out of epoxy resin, suitably coloured, or perhaps mixed with sawdust, and stick it in place.

There is no space here to expand on the techniques of woodcarving, but there are books in most local libraries on the subject.

To clean dirty woodcarving, give it a good brushing first with a stiff clean brush to get dust out of crevices. Remove grease spots with solvent. Wipe well with turpentine substitute. Don't wet woodcarvings or leave them in a damp place. Don't varnish woodcarving, for the varnish will tend to run and accumulate in the crevices. Brush a beeswax polish well into the wood. If necessary inject woodworm holes with Rentokil. Badly worm eaten woodcarving can be strengthened by the injection of epoxy resin into the holes, in the same way that gunstocks are treated. Paraffin wax will also seal up the holes, but does not strengthen the wood appreciably.

Wood Stains

All kinds and colours of wood stain can be bought, but it may be of some use and interest to have details of chemical stains and colourings.

To make mahogany stain, use bichromate of potash crystals dissoved in water. First make up a concentrated solution and then dilute it as required. When it is applied to the mahogany it darkens it considerably, and the depth of the colour can be controlled by the strength of the solution used. As the darkening only takes place as the wood dries, do not think you have not put enough on if nothing happens at first. It is best to test the colour on a spare piece of the same wood, before doing anything irrevocable.

Oak can be stained with Vandyke crystals. Dissolve in warm water and add a little ammonia 880 before applying it.

Aniline dyes in the appropriate colour dissolved in water or turps according to the type can be used for woodstaining. Vandyke Brown is suitable for oak. Bismark Brown makes a red stain, which is useful to warm up other stains. Black stain for ebony can be made with aniline dye.

Stripping paint and varnish from wood with caustic soda or ammonia will probably give wood a much darker colour than it has in its raw state, and this colour, if varnished or glazed, will remain fast.

MATERIALS AND TOOLS INDEX WITH SOURCES AND SUPPLIERS

Nothing is more annoying than to be told to use a certain material or tool, and then not to be able to buy it. I have tried hard to compile an accurate and up to date list of sources, with suggestions as to where you might be able to buy some of the more obscure materials. Unfortunately one is constantly met with the statement, in retail shops, that 'That stuff isn't used any more, only synthetics'. It is unavailing to point out that you don't want, for instance, to buy a whole tin of furniture stain to touch up a square inch of repair work, when you could make a teaspoonful of stain for yourself with the right chemicals. If you live in a big city you can probably buy most things, but if you live in the country, it may be harder. It is difficult to buy clock oil, locally, for instance, but a friendly chat with your local watchmaker, might yield a little bottleful, which is all you need. In other words you may have to ferret around a bit to find some of the items listed.

I must also point out that suppliers and firms go out of business for various reasons; at the time of writing, entries are correct, but in a year's time, there could be errors which I have no means of correcting once the book is printed.

Failing all else, Harrods of Knightsbridge claim to be able to supply absolutely anything, and the Army and Navy stores are also pretty good. Boots the chemists are most helpful and will try to get you anything in the chemical line.

Manufacturers are usually only too happy to answer any queries you may have on the uses and properties of their products, so do write to them direct if you have problems.

INDICES

MATERIALS AND TOOLS INDEX

SUBJECTS AND METHODS INDEX

NOTES

NOTES

NOTES

NOTES